Classroom Spaces That Work

Marlynn K. Clayton
with Mary Beth Forton

Introduction by Jay Lord

Illustrations by Linsey Doolittle

STRATEGIES FOR TEACHERS SERIES

All net proceeds from the sale of *Classroom Spaces That Work* support the work of Northeast Foundation for Children, Inc., a nonprofit, educational foundation whose mission is to foster safe, challenging, and joyful classrooms and schools, kindergarten through eighth grade.

The stories in this book are all based on real events in the classroom. However, in order to respect the privacy of students, names and many identifying characteristics of students and situations have been changed.

ISBN-13: 978-1-892989-05-5

ISBN-10: 1-892989-05-0

Library of Congress catalog card number 2001086281

Photographs: Peter Wrenn, Marlynn K. Clayton, Cherry Wyman, William Elwell, Apple Lord, Bonnie Baer-Simahk

Illustrations: Linsey Doolittle

Cover and book design: Woodward Design

NORTHEAST FOUNDATION FOR CHILDREN, INC.
85 Avenue A, Suite 204

P. O. Box 718
Turners Falls, MA 01376-0718

800-360-6332

www.responsiveclassroom.org

09 08 07 06   9 8 7 6 5

We would like to thank the Shinnyo-En Foundation for their generous support of the development of this book.

The mission of the Shinnyo-En Foundation is "to bring forth deeper compassion among humankind, to promote greater harmony, and to nurture future generations toward building more caring communities."

ACKNOWLEDGMENTS

This book grows out of my thirty years of experiences arranging and organizing classrooms. It also grows from the ideas of many educators who have contributed to *The Responsive Classroom®* approach to teaching and learning. Directly and indirectly, many of the words, ideas, pictures, and practices included in this book come from colleagues at Northeast Foundation for Children, Inc. and from educators in the field using *The Responsive Classroom* practices in their classrooms and schools. It is with deep gratitude and excitement that I share what I have learned over the years about the challenges and joys of making classroom spaces that work.

In particular, I wish to thank and acknowledge:

Mary Beth Forton, for her deeply respectful collaboration, for her gift of thinking and writing clearly and concisely, for her careful attention to detail in shepherding and editing this book, and for all the work she did to make it both useful and beautiful. I could not have completed this project without Mary Beth's steadfastness and skill in helping me think through and meet the challenges of writing, while at the same time making it fun.

My fellow Northeast Foundation for Children co-founders for their profound role in my growth as a teacher and classroom designer. Specifically,

Jay Lord, for his collaboration in the conception and shaping of this book, for his perceptive introduction, for his careful reading and feedback, and for his help with the illustrations. Also, Jay's inventive and playful approach to classroom design has always inspired me.

Chip Wood, for his deep support and appreciation of my work, for his commitment to creating spaces that work for children, and for his vital contributions to the chapter on children's development.

Ruth Charney, for her insightful understanding and gifted expression of what children need in order to be successful learners, and for her clear articulation and support of my skills in creating environments that make successful learning possible.

Roxann Kriete, director of the publishing branch of Northeast Foundation for Children, for giving me the opportunity to write this book, and for being an astute and insightful reader and editor.

Pam Porter, for her deep passion and insights about the complex connections between children's learning and their learning environment, for her thoughtful reading of this book, and for giving me the time to see this project to its completion.

Terry Kayne, for many years of generously and enthusiastically moving and painting the furniture and "stuff" in the classrooms we shared, and for her dedication to creating orderly and inviting classrooms that model the adage "less is more."

Deb Porter, for her ability to create and organize primary grade classrooms that demonstrate all that I believe is important for children's successful learning. I have learned so much from visiting her classrooms over the years.

Nancy Richard, for her incredible wealth of knowledge about child development, for our many conversations about designing effective classroom spaces for children, and for giving careful and constructive suggestions for Chapter One.

Paula Denton and Bonnie Baer-Simahk, for reading and giving so much helpful feedback on various chapters in the early stages of writing this book.

My colleagues serving as consulting teachers for NEFC—Eileen Mariani, Carol Davis, Pam Porter, Chip Wood, Ruth Charney, Susan Roser, Melissa Correa-Connolly, Bonnie Baer-Simahk, Sally Kitts, Beth Watrous, Paula Denton, Linda Crawford, and Marcia Bradley—for sharing information with me about the needs of classroom teachers, and for their commitment to creating classroom spaces that work.

Nancy Ratner, for her skillful and insightful editing at a time when it was greatly appreciated, and for her ongoing contributions to the work of the publishing branch of NEFC.

Alice Yang, for her clarity, her energy, and her thoughtful attention to detail, all of which she brought in great abundance to the job of copyediting the manuscript.

Michael Fleck, for the hours he spent gathering information for the appendixes, and for the care he brought to the task.

Jeff Woodward, for his careful proofreading of the manuscript, his consistently high standards, and his refreshing ability to make any job feel fun.

Leslie Woodward, for the many hours she devoted to designing this book, for caring so much about making it attractive and practical, and for being remarkably patient in the process of revision.

Linsey Doolittle, for her beautiful and lively illustrations, and for being so generous with her time and talents.

Peter Wrenn, for supplying so many photographs that capture the everyday moments of classroom life, and for sharing his skills with NEFC over the years.

Finally, I'd like to thank:

My parents, *Max and Esther Krebs,* for giving me the gift of believing in myself and the opportunity to learn the value of perseverance. My brother, *Tim Krebs,* for teaching me about courage and patience. And my mother, a special appreciation for sharing with me her love of creating beautiful, inviting, and practical spaces.

John Clayton and Sharon Dunn, my "extended" family, for their generous gifts of support and writing expertise through the years.

Garry Krinsky, my beloved husband, who supported, listened to, and believed in me through all the groaning and whining, and *Sasha Clayton,* my son, for showing his appreciation of his mom's knowledge and work.

I would like to dedicate this book to the many teachers who have allowed me to visit their classrooms and especially to those who have taken the risk of changing how they organize their classroom environments. What I have learned from each and every one of you has been inspiring and appears in many ways throughout this book.

Marlynn K. Clayton

APRIL 2001

TABLE OF CONTENTS

About *The Responsive Classroom®* Approach

This book has grown out of the work of Northeast Foundation for Children (NEFC) and an approach to teaching known as *The Responsive Classroom* approach. Developed by classroom teachers, this approach consists of highly practical strategies for integrating social and academic learning throughout the school day.

This approach has been defined, practiced, and revised with community passion for twenty years in the classrooms of Greenfield Center School, NEFC's K–8 laboratory school, in the workrooms of Northeast Foundation for Children, and in the halls, classrooms, and faculty rooms of the hundreds of elementary and middle schools across the country currently implementing this approach.

The book begins with a certain set of beliefs about teaching and learning. The following seven beliefs, based on developmental, cognitive, and social learning theory and informed by years of experience in the classroom, underlie *The Responsive Classroom* approach. (Wood 1999, 293)

The Responsive Classroom Beliefs

1. **The social curriculum is as important as the academic curriculum.**

   Social and academic learning are inextricably connected, and both are equally important. The balanced integration of the two is essential to children's growth.

2. **How children learn is as important as what children learn.**

   Children learn best when they have the opportunity to make choices about what they're learning and to make their own discoveries through trial and error. Ideally there should be a balance between teacher-directed and child-initiated experiences.

3. **The greatest cognitive growth occurs through social interaction.**

   Children certainly do learn when they are working alone (reading a book, taking a test, completing a worksheet, etc.). But they learn *the most* when they are engaged in meaningful interaction with others—when they are engaged in collaborative projects, small group and large group discussions, work sharings, peer critiquing, and partner work, for example.

4. **There is a set of social skills that children need in order to be successful academically and socially.**

   These skills form the simple acronym CARES—cooperation, assertion, responsibility, empathy, and self-control—and should be taught in an integrated fashion throughout the school day.

5. **Knowing the children we teach is as important as knowing the content we teach.**

   The more known children feel at school, the more likely it is that they will succeed. Teachers come to know children individually, culturally, and developmentally by taking time to observe and interact with students and by understanding the stages of child development. The science of child development is an essential academic discipline for teachers.

6. **Knowing the families of the children we teach is as important as knowing the children.**

   Family involvement is essential to children's education. The greatest gains are made when educators work with families as partners.

7. **Teachers and administrators must model the social and academic skills which they wish to teach their students.**

   These skills must be lived daily in educators' interactions with each other, with children, and with families. Meaningful and lasting change for the better in our schools requires good working relationships among the adult community. Children are always watching.

Introduction

**LESSONS FROM
THE APARTMENT CLASSROOM**

By Jay Lord, teacher and NEFC cofounder

In 1983, I taught a sixth, seventh, and eighth grade classroom of twenty-six children in a four-room apartment whose every corner was stuffed full. Like many classroom spaces in use today—portable classrooms, overly crowded classrooms, classrooms that are poorly designed or just don't fit their current uses—it was far from ideal. The apartment was located across the street from our K–8 laboratory school, which had become too small for our quickly growing enrollment. I had worked all summer to convert that apartment into what I hoped would be a suitable classroom space. Mostly, I focused on the details.

The computer went in the front room, the pet mice in the kitchen. The weekly world event map was secured to a wall. A round seminar table was rolled in for literature groups, and small clusters of desks were spread throughout where children could mull, think, and work. After much hammering, building, and moving, the details seemed to work. There was a space for everything that needed to be done.

Then the children arrived. It didn't take long, once I actually began using the space with twenty-six adolescents, to see all the flaws in my design. There were too many places for children to hide, there wasn't an adequate whole-group meeting area, it was impossible to keep clean, it was far too noisy, and it quickly became cluttered, to name just a few problems.

That year, my youngest child Hannah, at the time a first grader in the school, was given the assignment of getting to know the school, then building part of it in her classroom's block corner. As coincidence would have it, her job was to build my classroom. After several visits, many drawings, and interviews with the students, Hannah began building the apartment classroom with blocks. Her building not only captured the layout—the front door entering into a hallway, to the left the computer area, straight ahead the cluster of desks, another left into the kitchen—but also the details of each room. There were cardboard computers, desks made from small cubes, and little matchboxes to represent the mice cages that filled the kitchen counters.

After a full week of building, Hannah was quite proud of her work. As the last touch, she sat engrossed beside her structure carefully tearing up sheets of paper into hundreds of little pieces. Then she carefully showered her block structure with these tiny bits of paper until each surface in each room was covered. The clutter that so dominated the room in Hannah's six-year-old vision was now in place.

Details with No Direction

As I have thought about classroom space over the years, I have often come back to that room and Hannah's white paper clutter to remind myself of all that didn't work in that space. I now realize that I created each space as a detail without a plan that was informed by my knowledge and beliefs about children and learning. At the time, I didn't see the connection between what I wanted to teach these children, how I hoped they would learn, and the place in which we worked and lived together each day.

I had hoped to build a strong sense of community, yet the four separate rooms, none of which was big enough for all of us to sit together, drove us apart. I had hoped that the children would take pride in and care for their space, yet the clutter and the configuration of the space conspired against this. Every corner was jam-packed with "stuff," making cleaning difficult, not to mention the fact that the mice cages which needed to be cleaned every day were so far off the beaten track that they were quickly forgotten.

My intention to create quiet workspaces was challenged by the fact that every room served as a hallway to the next, resulting in a constant flow of traffic through most of the rooms. And my desire to make students feel safe from the adolescent social pressures that can so dominate a middle-school classroom was thwarted by the fact that there were walls everywhere that prevented me from seeing all of the children and offered far too many corners in which students could hide.

That classroom stood in direct contradiction to the intentions and the curriculum of the classroom. It didn't match my beliefs and knowledge of education, and as a result, the children were presented with mixed messages— what I said contradicted what the room said. This mismatch of room and curriculum, in addition to creating many daily problems, had an insidious side captured by Hannah's white paper clutter. The space got cluttered, jumbled, and too full. I blamed it on the children—The children were messy; The children were not taking care of the room; You know how they are, adolescents—when in truth, it was my classroom setup that was flawed, not the children.

A tension defined the room for most of the year—a discord that blanketed the room day-in and day-out. That discord kept the room from reaching its potential, made my work infinitely harder, and at times, made me angry with the children. How wrong I was. How little I understood.

Lessons to be Learned

During the past seventeen years, I've learned a lot about classroom spaces. I've learned to be more intentional and to look closely at the connections between how a classroom is designed and what happens within it. As I look at classrooms now, I ask teachers if their rooms are consistent with what they believe about teaching and learning. Are there reasons for the details of the room? What are the reasons?

Certainly, there will always be classroom spaces, like my apartment classroom, that are far from ideal. There will be spaces born of necessity, budget constraints, and bulges in school populations that will never be optimal. But even these less-than-ideal spaces, even my apartment classroom, could be made to work much better in the hands of a skillful teacher—one who understands clearly how room design impacts teaching and who has a repertoire of practical strategies for creating effective designs. The aim of this book is to help teachers develop this understanding and to provide them with these strategies.

This book will help teachers make the most of what they have to work with to create warm, orderly, and engaging environments that serve the needs of all their students. More concretely, it will help teachers to make informed decisions about where to place the desks, the books, the meeting area, the recycling bin, the collection of posters, the art work, the maps, the scissors, the paper, the storage shelves, the bookbags, etc.

These details matter. In fact, it is in the details that the classroom is defined. But the details, if they are to make sense, must get their direction from our strongest beliefs about education and children. A classroom that is not centered on educational beliefs is a room of disconnected details, a room of convenience rather than purpose. It is our focus on our educational beliefs that aligns all the details of the room, blending them together seamlessly to create the whole.

In San Francisco last year, I visited an exhibition of winter landscapes by the French Impressionists. As I approached "Snow at Louveciennes," a canvas by Alfred Sisley, I saw that it was a picture of an aproned woman with an umbrella walking slowly down a snow covered lane bounded by a stone wall and a wooden garden fence. Cottages dotted the hillside behind. Fascinated, I walked closer and closer to the picture until all I could see were thousands of small, quick strokes of color. The woman disappeared and the snow dissolved into these strokes.

Lessons to be Learned

Starting with Your Big Picture

It was these details, these small quick brushstrokes, that created this grand three-foot canvas, yet I knew that Sisley must have held a vision of the big picture in his mind as he created each one of them. It was this vision that gave each of the strokes its color, its direction, its placement. And it was precisely this vision that was so sorely missing in my apartment classroom. I've learned since then to always begin with the big picture when designing a classroom space. Before moving a table or lifting a hammer, I now ask myself, What are my most closely held educational beliefs? Why do I teach? How do children learn? It is the articulation of these educational beliefs that allows us to make coherent decisions regarding the thousands of details that create a well-designed classroom space.

Starting with Your Big Picture

We all have closely held personal beliefs about teaching which are likely connected to our reasons for becoming teachers in the first place. Ideally, these beliefs serve as a guiding force for all the decisions we make in the classroom. Ruth Charney, in her book *Teaching Children to Care,* talks about the importance of articulating a positive vision for one's teaching which is founded on personal convictions. Charney writes:

> As teachers, we need to know why we teach, and why we do what we do in the classroom. These ideals (or values) need to be conscious and clear. The process…begins by establishing the ideals, which become the foundations for our social arrangements and our expectations for content groups and individuals.

It is easy to lose sight of our ideals among the complex demands of every teaching day. If necessary, we need to go back and identify them again and again, recovering them from the piles of roll books, lesson plans and report cards—"the stuff" that may shroud our earliest spirit and most compelling desire to teach. When we truly know these ideals, we can use them to guide the specifics of our classroom. I know that we are all strongest as teachers when our ideals inform our teaching. (Charney 1991, 196)

Charney identifies her ideals as the following: schools need to teach alternatives to violence and to stress nonviolence as an essential characteristic of the community; children need to learn to think for themselves; educators need to stretch, not track, potentials. My ideals are different: we must value the voice of each and every child; we must, in a world of difference, be able to teach and practice empathy; we must equip every child with the necessary tools, both academic and social, to work and live with dignity. Your ideals will be different still. I suggest that you stop here and take a few minutes to think about and write down your ideals. What do you hope to achieve as a teacher? What is your guiding force?

While the details of our ideals need not agree, we must all begin with a positive vision as the foundation for our practice, a vision which is imbued with hope and possibility. This vision is highly personal and is the starting place for creating the classroom we want. We must be able to see and name what we hope for before we can realize it.

At their best, these ideals will translate into classroom practices that help children reach their potential both to learn well and to act in this world with compassion and kindness. My hope is that the ideas and strategies presented in this book—which you'll select, refine, and revise to best meet your purposes—will help you create a classroom that reflects your ideals and helps you achieve these ideals in your teaching. Best wishes for your journey.

Chapter One

Imagine spending every day in a space

designed for people much bigger than you. To wash your hands or get a drink
of water, you would need to drag over a chair or ask a friend for a boost. Your
feet would dangle in mid-air every time you sat down and you'd have to crane
your neck back and stand on tiptoe just to read the daily announcements on the
bulletin board. After the initial novelty wore off, it's likely that you'd feel
uncomfortable, insignificant, and strangely out of place.

Unfortunately, this is how many children feel every day in their classrooms.
Whether it's because the chairs are too big or too small, the aisles too narrow,
the tables too high or too low to write on comfortably, the displays placed far
above eye level, or materials difficult to reach, the message of the classroom setup
is clear: "This room was not made for you."

Imagine instead a classroom that says, "This room was created for you, with
your specific needs in mind, because you and your learning are important."

In a kindergarten classroom of exuberant five-year-olds, it might mean
that the teacher has removed furniture to make room for more large-muscle
activities like block building and water play. In a classroom filled with eleven-
year-olds who crave autonomy from teachers and interaction with peers, it
might mean that desks have been arranged in clusters with children choosing
where they will sit based on the kind of work they're doing. It might mean that
a private, quiet "office area" has been created for a child with attentional difficulties, or a table has been raised on blocks so that a child in a wheelchair can sit
and write comfortably.

I recently visited a second grade classroom where the chairs were far too high for most of the children. While the teacher wasn't able to purchase new chairs, she was able to supply children with simple wooden blocks which they kept under their chairs to use as footrests. This was a wonderful example of how a teacher's touches can sometimes make all the difference between an environment that alienates children and one that embraces them.

A footstool placed near the sink, a display placed at children's eye level, a cozy, quiet corner in which to read a book, a comfortable beanbag chair to sit in with a friend—all of these details, created by the teacher and based on his/her knowledge of children, are ultimately what work together to make children feel comfortable, significant, and at home in their classrooms.

Introduction

Over the course of the past thirty years—twenty years spent as a classroom teacher and ten years as a consulting teacher working in public schools nationwide—I have had a hand in setting up hundreds of classrooms and have seen just about every obstacle a teacher might face. I have worked in countless classrooms with inadequate storage, electrical outlets, bulletin boards, and counter space. I have worked in classrooms that are overly crowded and classrooms that are so big and empty that they give you the feeling of being in a warehouse rather than a schoolhouse. I have set up classrooms in basements with no windows, in rooms with no closets or walls, in trailers and other temporary spaces, and in "all-purpose rooms."

The sad fact is that most classroom spaces are far from ideal. Perhaps they were originally designed and built with little or no consultation with the teachers who would be working in them. Maybe they were designed for another purpose, or with tight budgetary restrictions.

While the barriers may sometimes feel insurmountable, the reality is that most teachers have no choice but to work with what they have. And while teachers probably won't be able to transform an inadequate classroom space into an ideal one, they can make dramatic improvements.

So, where to begin?

The most obvious place is by thinking about the students. Before moving a single piece of furniture or clearing a wall for a display, learn as much as you can about the particular needs of the children you'll be teaching. Since it's likely that you'll be setting up a classroom for a group of students whom you don't know yet, you'll have to begin by gathering information about them from families and former teachers.

In addition, you'll want to get a general sense of the overall developmental needs of the group. This will be addressed in detail later in this chapter.

Goals of Setting Up a Classroom for Students' Needs

There are essentially three goals to keep in mind as you arrange your classroom to best serve the children's needs:

- **The classroom should fit the range of physical sizes of the group.**

- **The classroom should accommodate children with special needs.**

- **The classroom should support students' developmental needs: emotional, social, cognitive, and physical.**

GETTING STARTED

Let's look at each of these goals individually as well as strategies for achieving them.

Make the Classroom Fit the Children's Bodies

While thinking about student size may seem too obvious a place to begin, I have learned through experience to make this an explicit part of the planning process. Too many times I have watched students struggle with attention and behavior problems that were clearly the result of being in spaces that were too small, too crowded, or otherwise unsuited to their physical sizes.

So, how do you go about considering size when setting up a classroom? The first step, before you even meet the students, is to estimate the range of sizes based on what's typical for that age. Next, use this estimate to:

- *Choose desks, tables, and chairs that fit the children.* This will not always be possible, but when choices exist, school furniture catalogs, which provide standard height and width calculations based on grade ranges, provide a useful resource. (See Appendix D for recommended sources of classroom furniture.) Also, as the earlier example of the footstools shows, with a little creativity you can make modifications to what you have to work with.

■ *Select and arrange freestanding bookcases and shelves in the classroom.* In general, children should be able to see and be seen over any set of shelves placed inside the perimeter of the classroom. Shelves that are taller than the students should be placed along the perimeter.

■ *Plan the amount of space needed for class gatherings or meetings.* When children are sitting in a circle or oval shape, there should be approximately three inches between each child regardless of whether children are sitting on the floor, in chairs, or on benches. By estimating the average size of each child and adding the amount of extra space needed for each child, you can plan fairly accurately for a comfortable and workable whole-class meeting space.

■ *Plan how to organize students for table work.* When children sit at a table to work, they need space for "elbow room" as well as a surface area on the table for their work and materials. Plan for this space in advance.

■ *Determine where to locate display areas and bulletin boards.* Displays meant for children's viewing and use should be at the children's eye level whenever possible.

■ *Plan enough space for the children to line up at the exit door.* To have children stand in line comfortably and safely, it is best to allow about nine inches between each child. By estimating, using the size of the children, the number in the class and the nine-inch rule, you can plan enough space for all children to line up in the room without bumping into obstructions or each other.

■ *Plan passageways—the aisles children use to move about the room.* In general, a passageway should allow two children to walk past each other comfortably.

After students arrive, reassess your plan by observing how the students use the room. During the first weeks of school, while teaching students how to work in the classroom environment, deliberately watch how they use the space and manage their behavior. Make necessary adjustments and, whenever possible, involve students in the process of resolving space problems that arise.

I once watched a fourth grade teacher do this very effectively during the first week of school. Lacking a space large enough to serve as a permanent whole-class meeting area, she decided to teach students how to move tables out of the way and bring their chairs into a circle for meetings. After teaching a process for doing this safely, the teacher allowed the children to practice on their own for a few days. Each day she asked the children to reflect on their progress in creating a clear, unobstructed circle in a timely and safe manner. Problems were acknowledged and solutions suggested, such as turning the tables sideways so that they would not intrude on the circle. Finally, after a few days of trying out various strategies and reflecting on their progress, the students and teacher decided together to relocate a set of file cabinets to a corner of the room in order to create the space they needed.

Inviting student involvement enlivens the process of classroom design, gives children a sense of ownership, and increases their cooperation and investment in making the design work.

Chapter One

Plan for Children's Special Needs

With more and more schools providing inclusion for students with special needs, it is essential that teachers consider how their classroom design will accommodate these children and help them feel a sense of belonging in the community.

The best place to begin is by having a conversation with the child, the child's family, and the team that is developing the child's education plan. In this way you can learn about the student's needs from many perspectives.

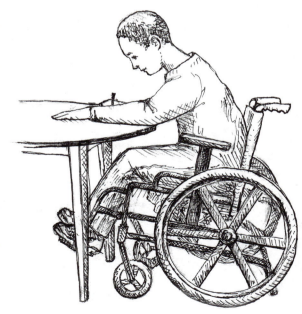

Depending on the child, adjustments may range from minor changes to major adaptations. A student in a wheelchair, for instance, might require additional space when sitting in a group or maneuvering around the classroom. A student who exhibits impulsivity might need two distinct work environments—one among classmates (at a table or desk group) and one by him/herself.

Having one or more one-on-one teachers aiding children with special needs will also impact the room design. Often, these teachers will need desk space of their own with access to special adaptive computers and materials.

There are excellent resources available on teaching children with special needs and making accommodations for them when designing classroom spaces. The Americans with Disabilities Act (ADA) Technical Assistance Program offers many excellent resources on their website: www.adata.org.

Finally, we all encounter students who are so much shorter, taller, or heavier than others that they need special accommodations to give them equal access to the classroom environment. Because these students often are already highly sensitive, teachers need to be flexible and creative in meeting their needs without drawing attention to them. Generally, simple measures can make a big difference for these students. Perhaps sturdy step stools can be placed beside shelves and work areas for short students, or chairs can be provided for everyone at circle time so that larger students can sit more comfortably without being singled out.

Consider Children's General Developmental Needs

While every child is unique, there are clearly predictable stages of development which most children go through. Take, for instance, the newly discovered independence of the two-year-old, the expansiveness of the six-year-old, the inward-looking tendency at seven, or the social awkwardness at eleven. Developmental theorists, like Piaget, Gesell, Erikson, Montessori, and Vygotsky, have taught us that as children grow, they pass through recognizable stages of development which teachers and families can come to understand and expect. While personality, life experience, temperament, and other factors all affect the rate at which children develop, most children pass through developmental stages in a fairly predictable fashion.

Understanding these patterns will help you to create effective classroom designs. In his book *Yardsticks: Children in the Classroom Ages 4–14,* Chip Wood asserts that "Children's developmental needs should be the foundation for every choice we make in our classrooms and schools. They need to remain at the center of our decisions about school organization, policies, scheduling, and everyday practices." (Wood 1997, 1) The critical question to ask yourself is "What are the general developmental traits I can expect from the group of children I'll be teaching?"

The first step is to determine the chronological age or cluster of ages, say, seven to seven-and-a-half, that represents the majority of students in your class. The birthday cluster exercise described on the following page will help you do this.

Of course, a single-grade classroom will always contain a wide range of chronological ages and, most likely, a span of developmental ages as well. In a multi-age classroom these spans double or even triple. While a teacher must meet the needs of every student in the class, knowing the dominant age of the students lets you make rough predictions about their range of developmental needs. Do you have a particularly young group of children this year? A particularly old group? Or a group with half of the children clustering in the young range and half in the older range? Gathering and reflecting on this information will allow you to be far more effective and efficient in creating and organizing a space that works for most of the children.

As the year progresses and you come to know students individually, you can make adjustments to best meet the changing needs of the group and the individuals within it.

**Chapter
One**

The Birthday Cluster Exercise

The birthday cluster exercise, developed by Chip Wood, offers one way for teachers to identify and organize information about the chronological ages of their students. It can give you a general sense of the developmental needs of a group of children and valuable insight into the behavior of individual children, especially those who fall outside the dominant age cluster.

The best time to do this exercise is as soon as you get your class list in the late summer. This will give you time before school begins to consider the developmental needs of the children in the group and organize the room accordingly.

As you do this exercise and consider the developmental ages and needs of the children in your classroom, it is important to keep in mind the following concepts regarding child development:

- *When a child moves into a new stage, it normally takes the child about three months to consistently exhibit the behavior of the new age.* For example, a child who turns seven in September will likely continue to exhibit some characteristic six-year-old behavior into December.

- *Not all children will pass through the developmental stages at the same rate.* Therefore, developmental age does not always match chronological age. A child might be ten chronologically but behave with characteristics more in keeping with a nine-year-old. If this behavior lasts more than three months into the new age, this child is most likely developmentally nine and needs to be treated differently than a ten-year-old.

The Birthday Cluster Exercise

Below are the steps to follow for the birthday cluster exercise. The samples on the following pages serve as illustrations of completed exercises from actual classes.

Step One: *List the students in the class by birth order from youngest to oldest.*

For each child identify the birth month, day, and year. Pay careful attention to the year of birth, particularly around the entrance cut-off date for your school. Based on the birth dates, list three more pieces of information beside each name:

- The chronological age in years and months on the first day of school
- The expected developmental behavioral age, taking into consideration the three-month lag described above
- The expected developmental behavioral age six months from the opening day of school

Step Two: *Identify the clusters of birthdays.*

Where do they fall? Is there a large cluster of summer birthdays, winter birthdays, or summer and spring birthdays with not many in between? This will give you important information about the developmental traits likely to appear in the class.

Step Three: *Anticipate the changes that will occur in the group's development over the course of the school year.*

Since children are growing all the time, teachers need to plan in advance for likely design changes. While many teachers put a lot of emphasis on arranging their classrooms in September, they often overlook the fact that students' developmental needs change throughout the school year.

Note: If it's already well into the school year, you can still switch from listing students alphabetically in your grade book to listing them by birth order. Most teachers who try this find it enlightening. Almost immediately they understand why some of their students behave in younger ways than the rest of the class!

Name	D.O.B.			Chronological age 9/6/00	Expected behavioral age 9/6/00	Expected behavioral age 3/6/01	
	M	D	Y				
Emma	8	26	93	7^0	6–7	7	①
Vaughn	8	23	93	7^0	6–7	7	
Suly	8	10	93	7^0	6–7	7	
Grace	8	8	93	7^0	6–7	7	
Mack	7	24	93	7^1	6–7	7	
Stephanie	7	15	93	7^1	6–7	7	
James	7	9	93	7^1	6–7	7	
Joshua	7	6	93	7^2	6–7	7	
Amelia	7	3	93	7^2	6–7	7	
Amanda	6	21	93	7^2	6–7	7	
Erika	6	12	93	7^2	6–7	7	
Austin	5	20	93	7^3	7	7	②
Zach	4	9	93	7^4	7	7	
Jeanette	4	9	93	7^4	7	7	
Connor	2	27	93	7^6	7	7–8	
Amanda	2	4	93	7^7	7	7–8	
Angel	1	13	93	7^7	7	7–8	
Oskar	12	30	92	7^8	7	8	
Olivia	12	28	92	7^8	7	8	
Lucas	11	5	92	7^{10}	7	8	
Alexander	10	26	92	7^{10}	7	8	
Jean	12	12	91	8^8	?	?	③
Emily	6	6	91	9^3	?	?	

Birthday Cluster Sample: Ms. T. Second Grade Class

1. There is a birthday cluster in the summer months, which means the class will be on the young side for second grade, with many children showing six-year-old behavioral characteristics in the fall. Ms. T. will arrange the classroom with a focus on meeting the needs of this younger group.

2. The remaining birthdays (with the exception of two) are evenly scattered through the spring, winter, and fall. While keeping the design of the classroom geared toward the younger group, Ms. T. will make modifications to meet the needs of these seven-year-olds.

3. Ms. T. will observe and find out more about these two children to understand their placement in this class and meet their needs.

In six months, when the majority of the group is showing solid seven-year-old behavior and a few children are showing eight-year-old behavior, Ms. T. will make changes in the classroom to meet the children's changing needs. The thrust of the changes will be focused on meeting the needs of the younger group.

Name	M	D	Y	Chronological age 9/6/00	Expected behavioral age 9/6/00	Expected behavioral age 3/6/01	
Ricardo	9	30	92	7^{11}	7	8	②
Jasmine	9	9	92	7^{11}	7	8	
Roque	8	31	92	8^{0}	7–8	8	
Daijsia	8	17	92	8^{0}	7–8	8	
Aisha	7	3	92	8^{2}	7–8	8	
Peace	6	21	92	8^{2}	7–8	8	
Hiko	5	6	92	8^{4}	8	8	①
Brittany	5	2	92	8^{4}	8	8	
Annie	4	30	92	8^{4}	8	8	
Allyson	4	20	92	8^{4}	8	8	
Jerard	4	2	92	8^{5}	8	8	
Juston	4	2	92	8^{5}	8	8	
Diana	2	24	92	8^{6}	8	8–9	
Julia	2	22	92	8^{6}	8	8–9	
Victoria	1	27	92	8^{7}	8	8–9	
Ebony	1	24	92	8^{7}	8	8–9	
Lisanna	1	10	92	8^{7}	8	8–9	
Elizabeth	1	3	92	8^{8}	8	8–9	
Guillermo	12	20	91	8^{8}	8	8–9	
Lisa	10	14	91	8^{10}	8	9	③
Danavian	10	3	91	8^{11}	8	9	
Carlos	5	3	91	9^{4}	?	?	
Hgozi	5	1	91	9^{4}	?	?	

D.O.B. spans the M, D, Y columns.

Birthday Cluster Sample: Mrs. L. Third Grade Class

1. There is a birthday cluster in the winter and spring months, which means students will be on the average to older side for a third grade class. Many children will be showing solid eight-year-old behavioral characteristics when they enter school in the fall. Mrs. L. will organize the classroom to focus on meeting the needs of eight-year-olds.

2. Mrs. L. will make adjustments for these six younger children who may still be showing seven-year-old characteristics in the fall.

3. These four children fall on the older side of the birthday cluster. The two children with October birthdays are in this class because their birthdays fell short of the school entrance cutoff date of October 1. Mrs. L. may need to make a few adjustments for them. She will observe and learn more about the other two older children to understand their placement and meet their specific needs.

In the spring Mrs. L. will make adjustments to the classroom to meet the changing needs of the class. During the latter part of the school year, the class will be showing more and more nine-year-old behavioral characteristics.

Key Growth Patterns and Implications for Classroom Setup Ages 4–12

The following charts offer a summary of the key developmental traits of children at different ages and the implications these traits have for classroom setup. The information regarding general growth patterns has been culled from Chip Wood's book, *Yardsticks: Children in the Classroom Ages 4–14*. For more information on children's developmental characteristics, see the recommended resources in Appendix E.

Chapter One

Four-Year-Olds

Key Growth Patterns

- Learn best through large-muscle activity

- Learn best through play, exploration, and physical activity

- Short attention span; learn best in small doses

- Vision is in the far field; not ready for much close-up work

- Gregarious and like working with others, though still often play in parallel with others

Four-Year-Olds

Classroom Setup Implications

- Classroom needs more open space than furniture. Limit amount of furniture, especially tables and chairs.

- Arrange furniture to create many open and spacious interest areas that allow groups of children to work together. Make sure furniture can be moved aside easily for large physical movement. Passageways around interest areas should be uncluttered and roomy. But avoid creating long, straight "runways" that invite children to run.

- Learning materials should require manipulation, exploration, and use of large muscles. Examples include blocks (big, hollow, or unit blocks, Legos, pattern blocks, etc.), puzzles, counting and interlocking math manipulatives, big books, picture books, stand-up easels for painting, markers, crayons, pencils, a sand and water table, puppets, and other dramatic play props.

- Limit the number of learning materials on a shelf or in an area, but change them regularly.

- Have displays that focus on big pieces of work—for example, group murals, easel paintings, and block constructions—for short periods of time (sometimes only for the day). Use photographs of the children working in various areas as displays. Change the photographs often.

Chapter One

Five-Year-Olds

Key Growth Patterns

- Active but gaining control over physical behavior

- Learn best through play and self-initiated action

- Repetition maximizes learning

- Vision is in the near field; ready for some close-up work

- Anxious to be "good" and "right"; like approval and rules

- Like to work with others in pairs or small groups

Five-Year-Olds

Classroom Setup Implications

- Arrange the room with defined learning/interest areas (Math Area, Block Area, Reading Corner, Listening Station, and Discovery Table, for example). All furniture, tables, and shelves in the classroom should be part of a learning area, not in addition to them.

- Low dividers around learning areas can be used to create closed-in, protected work places. However, make sure the dividers are low enough so children and teachers can make eye contact with each other from any spot in the room. Knowing they can be seen is essential for a five-year-old's sense of security.

- Clearly label learning areas and define the number of children who may use an area at one time in order to give a structure for success.

- Offer learning materials that invite active and concrete exploration. These could include blocks, manipulatives, paint, other art supplies, sand and water, and dramatic play props.

- Limit paper and pencil tasks and offer many choices of tools for writing— fat and skinny pencils, crayons and markers, unlined and lined paper, big and small sheets of paper.

- Clearly label all materials and their storage places.

- Make displays that are "language rich," using familiar and predictable language patterns that children learning to read can easily recognize. Create displays that feature a wide variety of work, encouraging children to take risks and try new mediums.

Chapter One

Six-Year-Olds

Key Growth Patterns

- Boisterous, sloppy, speedy; like to stand up and sprawl out to work

- Learn best through discovery; like process more than product

- Good visual pursuit but unable to shift back and forth from near to far vision, making copying from the black board developmentally inappropriate for most children this age

- Like new ideas, games of all sorts, artistic expression

- Competitive; can be bossy

- Socially enthusiastic; having lots of friends is important

Six-
Year-Olds

Classroom Setup Implications

- Furniture arrangement should support independence and new challenges in learning. Create an arrangement that offers plenty of open space for the six-year-old to sprawl and move about speedily while working. Not all tables or work surfaces need chairs and not all work surfaces need to be desks or tables. Desks can be grouped to make work areas for four to six children. Make clipboards available for working without a table or desk.

- Learning materials should invite active and concrete exploration, include a variety of games, and provide for broad experiences in the arts.

- There can be more paper and pencil tasks at this age, but it is critical that they are connected to active exploration. Offer a range of choices in writing tools and paper.

- Displays of work should change frequently and be "language rich." Create displays that show examples of "learning in progress" (for example, work that shows fixed mistakes, which draws attention to the process rather than the finished product) as well as some examples of quality final drafts.

Chapter One

Seven-Year-Olds

Key Growth Patterns

Seven-Year-Olds

- Like their privacy; like to work alone or with one friend

- Friendships shift very quickly

- Introspective, serious, moody, more reflective, easily distracted

- Visually nearsighted; written work is often tiny in size; still have difficulty shifting back and forth from near to far vision, making copying from blackboard developmentally inappropriate for most children this age

- Like working in confined spaces

- Like to review learning; perfectionistic; interested in details of how things work

- Need active exploration of concrete material for understanding, but ability to represent understanding symbolically is increasing

Classroom Setup Implications

- Furniture should be arranged so that children can work with partners or alone more often than in groups. Seating assignments should change regularly.

- Seven-year-olds often prefer individual desks to tables for work areas. They need spaces that offer privacy for working and for talking out "friendship" problems. Cardboard screens placed on desks can create such spaces.

- Most learning areas except for blocks and science should now be organized primarily as supply areas where children can get necessary learning materials and take them back to their individual spaces.

- Learning materials should still include many manipulatives, with an emphasis on small manipulatives, board games, puzzles, mazes, and codes. There should be plenty of opportunities for drama, science, and social studies discovery.

- Give lots of choices of art materials and writing tools. Offer many possibilities for symbolic and miniature representations of how things work in math, science, social studies, and language arts. Writing tools should include skinny pencils, replacement erasers to fit over used-up erasers, and lined paper.

- Focus displays on finished products, giving special attention to the display process. Create displays that show one "perfect" aspect in the product rather than overall perfection.

- Displays that provide concrete, specific rubrics for "perfection" (for example, an "Editor's Checklist" on the wall near the writing supply area) offer children a way to do self-checks comfortably.

- Create displays that document individual children's growth without comparison to others.

Chapter One

Eight-Year-Olds

Key Growth Patterns

Eight-
Year-Olds

- **Gregarious; like groups of friends; prefer same-gender activities**

- **Love to work cooperatively; most productive in group activities**

- **Vision becoming strong in near and far field, making copying from the blackboard possible now for most children**

- **Full of energy; tire easily but bounce back**

- **Gravitate towards forming "clubs" which can exclude others**

- **Very industrious but often exaggerate their own ability**

- **Have difficulty with organization**

Classroom Setup Implications

- Furniture should be arranged to create groups of desks or groups of children at tables. Change groups often to provide deliberate mixing of genders and friendships.

- Arrange furniture so it can be moved quickly and easily for whole-group "energy" breaks.

- Most learning materials should be provided in supply areas in the classroom.

- Make allowances for children who are younger and physically unable to copy from the blackboard. These children will be able to copy from a sheet of paper laid next to the paper they're copying onto.

- Continue to provide learning materials that allow for concrete, active exploration.

- Classroom materials should focus on helping children develop a multicultural and multiracial perspective and learn about the interdependence of communities.

- Learning materials should also include tools (such as planning and results forms, self-check lists for assignments and homework, etc.) that can help children to organize, plan realistically, and follow through with their plans.

- Displays should reflect the work of groups of children more than that of individual children. Display all children's work and draw attention to the value of diversity in the work displayed.

Chapter One

Nine-Year-Olds

Key Growth Patterns

- Increased coordination and control of fine motor abilities; fatigue easily

- Industrious; highly competitive; individualistic

- Worrier; anxious, negative

- Can work in groups but with lots of arguing; relationships center around interests

Nine-Year-Olds
- Like to work with partner of choice—usually a same-gender partner

- Greater intellectual curiosity

- Take pride in finished work; greater attention to detail

Classroom Setup Implications

- Organize the room so the furniture, primarily desks or tables, can be moved to create different groupings based on the purpose of the work and the interests of the children. Each grouping should have a distinct purpose—the grouping should last for as long as a project needs it, and then it should change.

- Arrange furniture so it can be moved quickly and easily for whole-group "energy" breaks.

- Make most learning materials available through supply areas in the classroom.

- Learning materials should reflect the shift from "learning to read" to "reading to learn." Have on hand lots of mysteries, biographies, nonfiction, and resources for beginning research tasks.

- Introduce many new tools for practice with "intense detail" work, such as calligraphy, embroidery, map making, and diagramming.

- Continue to provide materials for concrete, active exploratory experiences.

- Create displays that show the nine-year-old's capacity for in-depth study and for creating completed quality products. Competitive tendencies can be directed to self-evaluation by emphasizing patterns of growth in displayed work ("before" and "after").

- Use posters and signs created by children to add humor and lighten an atmosphere of negativity and worrying. (For example, I've seen playful posters created by third and fourth graders with the words "I can't" in the center of a circle with a bold, black diagonal line cutting through the words.)

Chapter One

Ten-Year-Olds

Key Growth Patterns

- Growth spurts begin

- Continued strengthening of fine motor skills

- Work very well in all kinds of groups; good at solving social issues

- Will do more gender mixing on their own

- Concrete organizational skills are at their height; classification skills and exactness are strong

- Increased ability to think abstractly

- Active, receptive learners; memory very strong

Ten-
Year-Olds

Classroom Setup Implications

- Design the room to allow for large cooperative groups and for children to pick places to work that fit their personal needs at the time. Places for quiet rest are still essential.

- Children can help to organize and label the classroom. They can help decide how to group desks or tables and how to use classroom space.

- Provide learning materials that emphasize the use of memory as a learning strategy for geography, all kinds of fact acquisition, spelling, math, singing, drama, and poetry and choral readings.

- Provide games and learning materials that are strategy and movement oriented.

- Provide tools that allow children to work with a focus on details; tracing, mapping, cartooning, and making comic books are all popular at this age.

- Create displays showing finished products that highlight individual and group competence. Displays can also highlight ten-year-olds' strength in memory and interest in collections.

Chapter One

Eleven-Year-Olds

Key Growth Patterns

Eleven-Year-Olds

- **Vast appetite for food and physical activity; in constant motion; often stressed**

- **Seek to belong; desire to form cliques is at its height**

- **Learn well in cooperative groups**

- **Not likely to do gender mixing on their own**

- **Love to argue and test rules; saving face is important**

- **Ready for new and demanding skills in cognitive arena; like work that feels grown-up**

- **Deductive reasoning advances but hands-on learning still critical**

- **Highly improved fine motor skills coupled with increased confidence in this area**

Classroom Setup Implications

- Arrange furniture so children can work together in groups often.

- Create groups with an academic purpose and change groups often, deliberately mixing genders and makeup of groups. Allow children opportunities to choose groups as well.

- Furniture should be easy to move to allow for physical activity indoors when necessary.

- Provide a private place for children to cool off when upset and/or to talk privately with the teacher or other children in order to work through social problems.

- Provide learning materials like a telephone and computer to help children do "real life" research.

- Provide materials which expose children to art, music, and handwork (such as sewing, weaving, and braiding). Children at this age are especially interested in learning new art forms and exploring delicate work (calligraphy, linoleum block printing, and Japanese brush stroke, for example).

- Plan for frequent food breaks during the day to help relieve stress, provide needed energy, and aid concentration.

- Displays should reflect effort, showing works in progress and highlighting intriguing questions from students' research and interviews. Displays should make explicit the connections between the children's work and adult work. Use displays to honor cooperative group efforts and validate diversity.

Twelve-Year-Olds

Key Growth Patterns

Twelve-
Year-Olds

- Frequent growth spurts; food and rest are very important

- Increased fine motor ability

- Peers more important than teacher; peers can help each other significantly with subject matter

- Will initiate own activity; self-awareness develops; adult personality begins to emerge

- High interest in current events, politics, social justice, pop culture

- Increased ability to think abstractly; research and study skills advance

Classroom Setup Implications

- Furniture arrangement should allow children to create the work areas they need—sometimes to work alone and sometimes with a group. Children need comfortable places to rest and read, as well as furniture and spaces for partner work and peer conferencing. Involve children in creating structures for organizing and cleaning up the classroom.

- Learning materials should offer opportunities to connect learning to the events and concerns of the real world. Newspapers, magazines, fiction with themes that tie into current events and social justice, and nonfiction that supports research in high areas of interest (such as the environment, history, economics, and social justice) are often effective learning materials. Library tools, adult tools for learning in science and math, and access to computers and word processing are essential.

- Materials for handwork and art expression are still important and necessary.

- Allow children to eat regularly during the day.

- Displays should highlight finished products that show children's depth of knowledge and acquired skills. Classroom displays can provide a place to recognize and celebrate children's accomplishments, competence, and growth into adult roles.

FINE TUNINGS

Q. *This year I will have a young child in my classroom who is legally blind and sees only light and dark shadows. He'll spend approximately half of his day in my room and have a one-on-one teacher to support his movement and help his learning by translating materials into Braille. What design implications should I consider?*

Fine Tunings

A. There are two significant space adjustments to consider. First, the one-on-one teacher may need a desk of her own. Second, the child will need a classroom design that allows him independence and inclusion in the classroom. One design solution I have seen work well in a situation similar to this is to place the child's desk and one other student's desk beside the one-on-one teacher's desk. These can be placed at the edge of the other students' desks and directly beside the meeting area. With this design the assisting teacher can work closely with the child, and the child has a partner like everyone else. The child can maneuver around his desk, the friend's desk, and the teacher's desk, as well as to and from the meeting area, all on his own. In addition, when the child who is blind is not in the classroom, the friend can easily move his/her desk to join another grouping. An older child who has received mobility training or a child with less severe sight loss may be able to manage with significantly less accommodation.

Q. *I will have a child who uses a wheelchair in my classroom next year. What design adjustments should I make to help this child feel included in the classroom?*

A. You can help this child in a number of different ways. Place materials and displays at a level that will be easily accessible from the wheelchair. Make sure passageways will accommodate the width of the chair and ask students to sit in chairs at the whole-class meeting area so everyone will be at a similar height. Most important, consult the student, the student's family, and the education team to learn how best to support the student's independence and success in the classroom.

Q. *I teach second grade and have always asked students to copy homework assignments, spelling words, and math problems from the blackboard. I recently learned that not only is this physically impossible for many children until at least the age of eight, but it can also be harmful to the development of children's eyes. Can you tell me more about this and what I can do instead?*

A. According to research on children's vision done by Dr. Arnold Gesell, Dr. Frances L. Ilg, and Glenna E. Bullis (*Vision: Its Development in Infant & Child.* Santa Ana, CA: Optometric Extension Program Foundation, 1998), the muscles of the human eye are not fully developed until around the age of eight. Until then, these muscles are not capable of making the shifts from far-to-near and near-to-far that copying from a blackboard, chart stand, or wall demands. Asking children to make these shifts can actually do harm to the developing eye muscles.

However, children eight and under can copy from a sheet of paper laid next to the paper they're copying onto. This kind of "side-by-side" copying does not require a visual shift and will not hurt their eyes.

Children can also do side-by-side copying from a small chalkboard or a small dry erase board that's set down flat next to their paper. You might want to make several "originals" which children can then share to complete copying assignments.

Chapter One

Finally, I've seen teachers who have "word walls" address this issue by attaching the word cards to the wall with Velcro, pushpins, or hooks. Students can then easily remove the words for side-by-side copying. Another option is to create two or three additional sets of words, alphabetically organized and stored near the word wall, which students can use for copying.

Chapter Two

A PLACE FOR EVERYTHING AND EVERYTHING IN ITS PLACE

I*t's mid-morning in a second grade classroom and language arts has just begun. Students have recently finished a series of Frog and Toad books and are excited to begin book projects. Some have chosen to write their own stories about friendship, some to work with a partner to make paintings or dioramas of favorite scenes from the books, and others to work with a small group to put on a play. After a brief planning meeting, students eagerly scatter to their work areas. The drama group meets with the teacher at the rug to discuss roles. Children writing stories collect notebooks and pencils and quickly settle into their writing at a group of tables.*

But nearby in the art area, things do not go as smoothly. Ellie and Kyle search through a jumbled drawer of art supplies in various states of disrepair, looking for a jar of green paint which Ellie insists "was right there last week." Tameka and Travis rummage through a nearby storage shelf, equally jumbled, looking for glue and cardboard. After several minutes and no success, the four children abandon their search in favor of a playful game of poking, giggling, and hiding behind the storage shelves. As the noise level rises, students in the writing area begin hushing the students in the art area and shouting at them to "Be quiet!" The rising tension and commotion eventually catch the teacher's attention, pulling him away from his work with the drama group. Irritation visible on his face, he makes his way over to the art area, all the while vowing to himself that this is the last time he'll offer children choices for their book projects.

Little can be taught or learned in a classroom without order. If a classroom feels disorganized and cluttered, if supplies are in disrepair or can't be found, if children can't concentrate or easily move around the room without bumping into furniture or colliding with each other, then learning will be compromised.

In the example above, it didn't take long for the lack of order in just one area of the classroom to impact the entire room, shifting the mood from one of excitement and investment to one of frustration. A classroom that is disorganized and disorderly not only sends the negative message that no one cares about the space, but the clutter and chaos will inevitably interfere, as they did in this case, with classroom management and every aspect of teaching and learning.

Children need a classroom environment they can understand and trust. They need to understand the routines and to know where to find things, they need uncluttered spaces to do their work, and they need clear, safe pathways for moving about. It's essential that classrooms be well organized, predictable, and orderly, with a place for everything and everything in its place. Not only will this make the classroom pleasant to be in, but it will nurture children's initiative and creativity, enable them to use and care for the space independently, and clearly communicate the message that this is a space worth caring about.

Goals of an Orderly Classroom

Goals of an Orderly Classroom

Essentially, an orderly and predictable classroom will:

- **Facilitate classroom management, helping teachers to manage the classroom with ease and consistency**

- **Promote students' sense of independence and self-reliance**

- **Help students make purposeful choices and maintain focus, which fosters initiative and maximizes learning**

- **Encourage orderly behavior, care of materials, and care of work areas**

- **Create a sense of safety and security, so children are more likely to take risks in learning**

There's no one right way to create an orderly and predictable classroom. What's most important is that you create systems of organization that make sense to you and to the children, that you teach the systems well, and that you are vigilant about keeping the room and the materials organized and in good working order.

GETTING STARTED

When trying to organize an entire classroom space, it can be difficult knowing where to begin. The first step is to release yourself from feeling that you need to accomplish everything on your first try. Instead, choose one or two areas to focus on. Once you see the benefits of your efforts in these areas, it's likely that you'll be eager to do more. Below are some strategies and suggestions to help you get started.

Limit the Amount of Furniture and Materials

In my twenty years of working with teachers on classroom setup, one of the biggest problems I see is too much furniture and too many materials.

As the result of being on tight budgets, many teachers, myself included, feel that they need to hoard the items they have. In fact, many of these items never get used, or get used only once or twice, while their presence makes the classroom feel cluttered and congested. There's an old adage that I keep in mind when organizing a classroom: *Less is more.* Here are some reasons why:

- *Too much furniture creates safety hazards.* Children are more likely to trip, fall, or collide with each other or the furniture when moving about the room.

- *Too much furniture crowds students together.* This makes it difficult for children to behave positively and purposefully. Over and over, I see classrooms in which cluttered, overcrowded spaces are the direct cause of behavior problems. When children are confined to spaces that are too small, or when they don't have enough room for making transitions without bumping into each other or the furniture, the inevitable result is increased tension, conflict, and misbehavior.

- *Too much furniture makes the room difficult to clean.* Cleaning becomes a challenge for the students, the teacher, and the custodians.

- *Too many available materials can make the environment overly stimulating.* This can make it difficult for students to make purposeful choices and focus on their work. Cluttered rooms lead to cluttered minds.

- *Too many materials can lead to safety hazards.* For example, storage shelves that are overflowing, that have items sticking out or falling to the floor, can result in cuts, scrapes, and bruises.

Chapter Two

Deciding What's Essential:
Criteria for Furniture, Materials, and Storage Space

Deciding exactly which materials and furniture to keep and which to discard, recycle, or place in long-term storage can be difficult. While there isn't a specific formula that can be applied to every classroom, there are some general criteria that can help.

Furniture

General criteria for furniture:

- All furniture should have at least one clear purpose—and preferably more than one—that is relevant to children's development and the curriculum.

- All furniture should be actively used for some part of each day—and preferably for most of each day.

- Children should be able to move safely and easily around any furniture in the room.

- All furniture should be easy to clean and allow for easy cleaning of the room.

- All furniture should be in good condition and be safe for children to use.

Any furniture that has no clear purpose should be removed. If a piece of furniture has only one purpose or is used only once or twice a day, explore whether another piece will get more use. If a piece of furniture is clearly needed but is in poor condition, is unsafe, or creates traffic or cleaning problems, replace it with something safer and more convenient.

Materials

General criteria for materials:

- All materials should have a clear purpose that is relevant to children's development and the curriculum. It's best if the same material can be used for more than one topic or activity.

- All materials should be used at least every two years.

- All materials should be in good condition and be safe for children to use.

Get rid of materials that don't have a clear purpose. If any material is used infrequently, consider replacing it with another kind of material that will get more use. If materials that are clearly needed and frequently used are unsafe or in poor condition, get newer and safer replacements for them.

Chapter Two

Storage Space

General criteria for storage space:

- The criteria listed above for furniture apply to storage space as well.

- Every child should have at least one individual storage space, and preferably two spaces—one for learning materials and one for personal belongings such as backpacks and coats.

- "Teacher-controlled" storage space (storage that is accessible to the teacher, but not to children) should consume no more than a quarter of all available storage. If it consumes more, consider storing some teacher materials at home or create a teacher resource shelf in the teachers' room or the school library.

Consider adding more storage if there isn't enough to store materials in a neat, safe, and easily accessible way, or if you frequently use children's storage space for overflow teacher materials.

Arrange the Furniture So You Can See the Entire Classroom and Everyone in It

The arrangement of the furniture and space must allow the teacher, no matter where s/he is in the room, to see all the children, no matter where they are in the room. This means there should be no high bookcases or other obstructions in the middle of the room and no corners that invite hiding.

Implicit in this design is the message, in the words of Ruth Charney, author of *Teaching Children to Care,* "I see you. I see everything." (Charney 1991, 19) A classroom designed for optimum observation provides the children with a sense of safety, maximizes the teacher's ability to facilitate learning, and promotes responsible, productive behavior.

As pieces of furniture are put into place, move to different parts of the room and try out the view. First do this standing up. Then, in areas where you know you might be sitting for periods of time, try the view from a seated position. However, wait to make a final determination until the children are in the room. Only then will you be able to give your view the real test!

Arrange the Furniture

Cluster Work Areas

Cluster Work Areas Deliberately

Deciding where student work areas should be is critically important in arranging a classroom. You'll want to locate work areas in places that will encourage positive behavior and productive work. To do this, think carefully about the kind of work and behavior you expect in each work area. Then cluster work areas that are compatible. While this may be difficult in a small or crowded classroom, it's an important goal to aim for. Here are some ideas to consider when clustering work areas:

- *Quiet vs. noisy work*

  When students are working on a collaborative project or playing a game, the talk and movement will generally be lively and productively noisy. To allow for the noise, these work areas should be clustered together and as far away as possible from quieter workspaces. If, for example, the art area is too close to the quiet reading area, students trying to read may not be able to concentrate and may start to show inappropriate behavior.

- *Fragile vs. nonfragile work*

  When students work on fragile or delicate projects, such as models, block structures, large multi-pieced puzzles, and science or math experiments, they need to work where their projects cannot be damaged. Whether this type of work occurs regularly or only periodically, you should plan a work area that is protected from the normal classroom traffic and activity. For example, younger students, particularly those in kindergarten and first grade, often need a designated area for block building that is protected on at least three sides, and sometimes four, and has a single entrance/exit. This allows the students to build confidently without fear that someone walking through might cause damage to their structures. When students embark on a long-term project, a table or desk large enough to hold the project-in-progress and all the loose pieces should be set up in a part of the classroom where there's no danger of pieces getting rearranged, lost, or knocked to the floor.

- *Private vs. whole-community areas*

  Students have a need for privacy in the classroom. Ideally there will be a place for students to be alone, a place where two or three students can talk about a problem, and a conference area where students can speak privately with the teacher. All of these are best located near a quiet working area where only a few students congregate at a time, such as the class library, the computer area, or the teacher's desk. Another option is to use a seldom occupied corner of the room. Avoid passageways and areas where students tend to congregate, such as the class meeting area, the coat closet, the sink area, areas among desks, and areas near exits.

- *Messy vs. neat areas*

  Plan to have students do messy work where the mess will not interfere with other work and will preferably be out of the way of regular traffic. When students are working on messy art projects, particularly those that involve paint or water, make sure their work area is not near classroom materials such as books, games, or maps that could be ruined by spills.

- *Work area vs. traffic path*

  In general, work areas should have traffic coming to them but not through them. Remember the places in a classroom that draw constant traffic, like the bathroom and sink area, the exit doors, and perhaps the coat area, and avoid using the spaces in front of them as work areas. For example, there will be a constant flow of traffic through the meeting area if it is in front of the bathroom entrance. This traffic will disturb any whole-group meeting or small-group teaching that takes place in the area, as well as any individual or partner work spread out on the floor.

Provide a Personal Space for Every Child

It's essential that there is space in the classroom for children to keep their school-work and personal items. This keeps the classroom organized and provides children with a sense of security and belonging. There are many ways of creating personal storage space. Here are a few of the most common:

- Individual closet hooks with floor space below and/or shelf space above for coats, backpacks, lunchboxes, boots, extra clothing, etc.

- Cubby holes for personal belongings from home and/or school. These are usually plastic bins stored on shelves or in units designed to be cubbies.

- Work pockets for holding academic folders, notebooks, and texts (see illustration on left). These are made out of canvas or heavy denim in two styles. One is sewn as a flat hanging, incorporating a group of pockets (generally four to eight) and placed on a wall or back of a shelf or bookcase. The other style is sewn as an individual pocket and hung on the back of a child's chair (see photo).

- Desk drawer for folders, notebooks, and texts.

Plan for Safe and Smooth Traffic Flow

Well-designed traffic pathways can help students to move around the classroom safely, easily, and responsibly. This can improve transitions, help children to establish self-control, and generally support a productive and cooperative learning environment.

As you plan pathways, the first step is to anticipate the natural traffic patterns that will occur in the classroom. The following Traffic Flow Exercise will help you to do this.

Traffic Flow Exercise

Draw a simple diagram of your classroom. Then use arrows to mark students' movements in the classroom during different periods of the day and for different kinds of work. To do this, consider the following:

1. The shortest distance between areas of activity—This is the path that students will most naturally follow.

2. The parts of the room between which there is naturally the most movement—For example, between the meeting area and the students' desks or tables, the meeting area and the exit doors, the students' desks or tables and the coat closet, and to and from the bathroom and the sink.

3. The places that draw a lot of traffic due to the students' high interest—These include the meeting area, the bulletin boards, classroom animal areas, and shelves containing the most commonly used materials.

Chapter Two

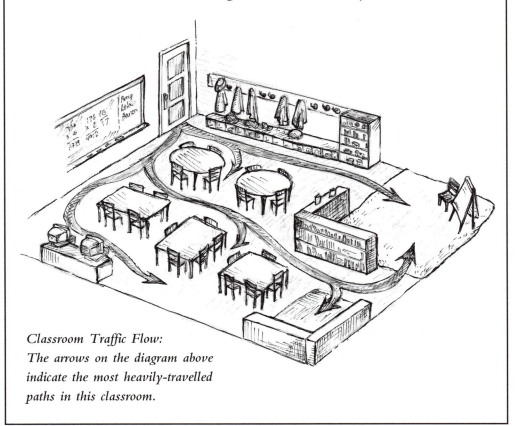

Classroom Traffic Flow:
The arrows on the diagram above
indicate the most heavily-travelled
paths in this classroom.

Traffic Path Guidelines

Below are some general guidelines to follow when planning pathways.

- *Whenever possible, design paths that allow students to take the natural, logical, shortest route between areas of activity.* This will make it easier for students to move appropriately through the classroom.

- *Make all paths wide and unobstructed, providing ample space for students to pass by one another.* Allow room for natural obstructions such as chairs sticking out from desks when students are sitting in them. Other obstructions which require extra width might include storage bins sticking out from shelves, angled chair or chart legs, and the edge of a carpet.

- *Protect the areas of fragile work by redirecting traffic paths around them.* Also design the paths into the area to ensure that only a few students can enter at a time and that their entrance won't disturb work.

Traffic Path Guidelines

- *Create boundaries to redirect undesirable pathways.* Examples of things that make good boundaries include bookcases, two desks side by side, stackable crates, low file cabinets, and freestanding bulletin boards or flip charts. Tables or desks can make good boundaries, although primary-age students are often tempted to crawl under them.

  To be effective, boundaries must be:

  Sturdy: They won't fall over and can't easily be moved.

  Solid: They form a solid blockage and aren't, for example, simply a rope that children can duck under.

  Obvious: They are high enough to be within approaching students' visual field but low enough so the children and teacher can see over them.

- *Prevent bottlenecks in areas of heavy use or high interest.* There are a variety of ways to do this:

  1. Make many paths into heavily used areas, such as the meeting area, so that all students can quickly and easily move into or out of the area at the same time.

  2. Strategically place the paths so they feed the incoming traffic to different parts of the area and the outgoing traffic to different parts of the classroom.

  3. Locate high interest areas, such as supply shelves for commonly used materials, in different parts of the classroom. For example, instead of putting all the writing portfolios in the same file box, put them in three

different areas of the room. Similarly, you might place three separate shelving units, each holding math manipulatives, in different parts of the classroom with traffic paths leading to each one from the students' desks and the meeting area.

4. In the case of high interest areas that involve very limited space, such as a single bulletin board or a chart stand, create a plan for a measured traffic flow in and out of the area. Students are often helpful in coming up with such plans. Perhaps a certain number of children are allowed in the area at one time, or the item of high interest is moved to another area which will accommodate more students. Whatever the solution, the goal is to maintain a safe and comfortable flow in and out of the area.

5. When necessary, stagger the release of students from high use areas. Teachers of younger children often do this in playful ways that also provide students with opportunities to practice categorizing. ("All the children wearing blue today may leave the circle." "Anyone who has just one pet may line up at the water fountain.")

Make Materials Accessible and Easy to Use Responsibly

In arranging learning materials, the goal is to make them as accessible as possible and to encourage students to use them independently and responsibly. Here are three ways to do this:

Clearly label materials intended for student use and store them at eye level or below.

Consider carefully what materials students will use independently and clearly separate them from materials you wish to keep in your control. Arrange materials meant for independent use in places that are within every student's reach. Label the storage places, with words and/or graphics, so students will have a constant, visual reminder of the learning materials they may access independently and will know where to return materials when they are done.

While clearly labeling materials provides children with a sense of comfort and fosters self-reliance, it's important not to overuse this technique. If every possible item and surface is covered with labels, children will be overwhelmed by the dizzying hodgepodge of words and graphics.

Place all the materials you do not want students to use independently in areas that are not accessible to them. In many classrooms, this kind of storage space is at a premium. If you don't have storage closets or shelves out of the reach of students, here are a few effective alternatives:

- *Covered boxes*—cardboard boxes or banker's boxes covered with colorful contact paper or painted to blend in with the room
- *Stacking plastic boxes with lids*
- *Homemade curtains to hide an open shelf or a low shelf*
- *Signs marked "For Teacher Only"*

The critical point is to provide students with a clear, visual understanding of what materials are meant for their independent use and what materials are off limits.

Make Materials Accessible

Place learning materials near the workspace where they will be used.

Put messy art materials, like paints and clay, near the areas designated for that kind of art work. Place science materials for experiments or projects near the areas designated for science work and display. Store clipboards near the carpeted meeting area where students will most likely use them. While this might seem obvious, I emphasize it because I've often seen poor placement of materials result in conflicts, mishaps, and wasted teacher and student energy.

Students should be able to access necessary materials quickly and efficiently. Strategic organization of materials cuts down on students' preparation time and eliminates potentially hazardous situations, such as students walking across a room carrying paints, water, or armloads of materials.

Avoid placing learning materials in or near areas that might lead to their unsafe or inappropriate use.

I have often seen students use materials inappropriately simply because the design of the classroom made it easy or tempting to do so. Here are some examples of how design problems can lead to behavior and management problems:

The exit—When classroom tools such as markers, scissors, or staplers are located next to the exit, they can create problems ranging from the annoying to the seriously dangerous. For example, when students line up at the door, if the line goes beside the classroom tools, students may be tempted to fiddle with the tools while waiting. This may invite a constant struggle between the teacher and students. On the more serious side, an angry student leaving the classroom could easily and even secretly grab a sharp implement and intentionally do some harm.

The sink—In early-childhood classrooms (pre-K to first grade) where exploration and experimentation serve as the main road to learning, teachers should be careful about placing learning materials near the sink. One common pitfall involves the sand and water table. Thinking it would be convenient to empty water into the sink, teachers often place the sand and water table beside the sink. This ignores the child's natural inclination to experiment with water when it is nearby. A big mess can result if a child adds water to a table filled with sand or beans.

The meeting area—In classrooms where there is a designated meeting area, teachers often store learning materials on the shelves that create meeting area boundaries. This works well except when the learning materials are exposed in open containers or are easily accessible. During meetings held in this area, many children, but particularly those with attention difficulties, will struggle to keep their hands out of the inviting learning materials.

Chapter Two

Keep the Design Predictable

Students need a learning environment they can trust. An environment that constantly changes, particularly without warning, can make students feel insecure and undermine a sense of group ownership. It's best if the classroom design that greets students at the beginning of the year stays unchanged, except for minor adjustments, at least through the first six weeks of school as students are becoming acclimated to a new environment.

When changes do become necessary throughout the year, plan them with care, making sure they are well thought out and that the timing is right. Many teachers involve students in the process of making design changes in the classroom. At the very least, teachers should talk with students in advance about any design changes that may occur in the classroom.

FINE TUNINGS

Q. *I write the morning message on the meeting area chart for students to read when they first enter the room. However, I find we have terrible crowding and arguments as students all try to read the message at the same time. Some cannot see it and others have to wait a long time for a turn to write their response to questions. What do you suggest?*

Fine Tunings

A. I recently saw an example of this in a second grade classroom. All the students arrived at the same time in the morning and all were excited to read their teacher's morning message as soon as they entered the room. The crowding, pushing, and arguments were atrocious. Recognizing that the problem was primarily one of traffic flow, the teacher designed a measured traffic flow plan with the children's input.

They decided that four students could comfortably and safely fit at the chart. Each day on a rotating basis four students would be named the first to go to the chart when they arrived in the morning. When they were done, it was their responsibility to pass to other classmates the markers they used to answer the teacher's question. This signaled those classmates' turn to go to the chart. Those students in turn would do the same until all classmates had had a turn. This resulted in a safe, comfortable, and measured flow to and from the chart.

Q. *I would like to introduce several major changes to my classroom, including moving the meeting area and the surrounding bookshelves to make room for students' growing bodies. How do I ensure these changes go smoothly?*

A. Two things to consider are how dramatic the change is and how much you plan to involve the children in helping to make the change. Whenever I make a large mid-year change (such as rearranging the placement of a work area, moving the meeting area, or changing a theme study), I ask the children to help even if I had not involved them in deciding to make the change. Large changes usually entail reorganizing materials, a golden opportunity to clean house. Therefore, you might choose to begin sorting through materials before the planned change.

As you think about how the change will occur, gather ideas from the children. Then choose a Thursday afternoon to make the change. Allow one or two days before moving the bookshelves for children to empty books out of them into crates or boxes, and give yourself time after school to do any work that the children cannot do. You will have all day Friday to try out the new arrangement. The weekend provides an important break for you and the students before continuing to adjust to the changes the following week. It also gives you time to deal with any problems that you might still need to address.

Q. *I want to use a nonverbal signal in my classroom to get children's attention when I make an announcement or give a direction. I've been trying a "lights out" signal. However, it's hard to use this signal consistently because of the location of the switch, and even when I do use it consistently, it's not as effective as I had hoped. Do you have any suggestions for making this technique more effective?*

A. A nonverbal signal, such as a raised hand, a bell ring, or lights out, can be a helpful tool for managing a classroom, but the location of the signal is important to its success.

Chapter Two

If the light switches are located near the door and away from the main activity, this will make it difficult for you to use the lights out signal effectively. I suggest you teach students several nonverbal signals so you can choose the one that best fits a given situation. For example, when children are sitting in a meeting or in a small group, a simple raised hand can be the most effective signal for quiet. When children are scattered throughout the room, however, an auditory or lights out signal will work better. If you decide to change your signal, be sure to give the children lots of time to practice with the new signal before expecting perfection!

In any case, it's important to have quick, easy access to the signal. If you're using a chime, for example, place it in a central part of the classroom with open pathways to it. In many classrooms teachers place a chime or bell near the meeting area because it is close to the central activity of the classroom. Another possibility is to have more than one bell or chime in the classroom, strategically placed near the most active areas of the room.

Q. *This summer I took a course and learned about a discipline strategy called "thinking time," a positive use of time-out. I'd like to start using this strategy but would like some guidance about the best placement and design for an area for thinking time. Can you help?*

A. Thinking time can be a useful and positive strategy for helping children regain self-control. However, time-out is a complex strategy, and one needs a thorough understanding of its purpose to use it effectively. For those interested in learning more about positive uses of time-out, I recommend *Teaching Children to Care* by Ruth Charney and *Positive Discipline* by Jane Nelsen.

In answer to your question, the physical location and setup of the place where children go for thinking time is key to making this strategy work. Below are four basic guidelines that should help.

1. It is essential that the classroom have at least two designated, permanent spots for thinking time which are never used for any other purpose.

2. The placement of these two spots is important. They should:

Fine Tunings

- Be in the classroom, never outside the classroom, so that a child feels the safety and security of being seen by the teacher. A child who is working to regain self-control may not have enough self-control at the moment to appropriately manage his/her behavior alone or even to remain in a hallway.

- Be in a quiet part of the room but not isolated in a corner or behind a tall file cabinet. Isolation will make a child feel alienated, and too much surrounding activity will be distracting.

- Be visible to the teacher from anywhere in the classroom so the teacher can ensure that the child is meeting expectations for thinking time behavior.

- Be in an uncluttered space, away from learning supplies and other materials that might be tempting. Placing a spot for thinking time directly next to open bins of math manipulatives, for example, demands too much from a child who is already struggling with self-control.

3. What children sit on for thinking time can make a difference in their perceptions of this strategy. I suggest seating that is comfortable and doesn't feel punitive. There are many possibilities, ranging from a simple student chair or a small rug on the floor to a comfortable bean bag chair. I encourage you to talk with students about what furniture they think would work best for thinking time.

4. While you don't want too many distracting materials near the area for thinking time, there are a few items that can be useful. Many teachers display a concise, student-generated list of helpful hints for regaining self-control (for example, count to fifty, take five deep breaths, think of some-

thing you love to do, etc.). Teachers of older children often display a poster or two of a relaxing scene—a sunny beach, a waterfall, a mountain vista. Other teachers set up a basket with several items that might help children relax, such as a soft stuffed animal, a "kneading egg" for stress release, or a piece of soft clay.

Q. *I work in an open space school where I teach with five other teachers in a "pod" with no built-in walls between our areas. The physical setup of our space presents many challenges in terms of noise and competing levels of activity. Do you have any suggestions?*

A. Open space schools do indeed present many challenges and will always be problematic for those attempting to teach in a self-contained format. Open space schools were designed with the idea that all six teachers would be working together as a team, with different learning activities occurring in each area of the pod. Class sizes were intended to be small enough that the noise would be manageable.

Chapter Two

Today, class sizes are too large for this model, and while some teachers in open space schools do try some team-teaching, the high numbers of children and the responsibilities of each teacher make team-teaching extremely difficult for most.

Although they will not provide a perfect solution, many of the ideas described and illustrated in this chapter will certainly help you meet the challenges of your open space building. In addition, here are two ideas that others in your situation have found helpful:

1. Consider the spaces adjacent to yours when you plan your room. For example, make sure that you and the adjacent teachers situate your whole-group meeting areas on opposite sides of your classrooms. Try to locate your quiet areas next to the quiet areas of the adjacent classrooms. Do the same with the noisier areas. Another possibility is to coordinate with adjacent teachers so that noisier and quieter activities occur at the same time of the day. This is not a panacea but it will definitely help.

2. If you do work as a team with another teacher, plan your spaces as one large space. However, it will still be important to be able to meet separately with the children who are considered your class and to make other smaller group configurations. Therefore, as in the above example, be careful to locate meeting areas away from each other to minimize competing noise.

Chapter Three

THE WHOLE-GROUP MEETING AREA

Come join in the circle, there's room for everyone...," *softly sings Ms. Ross, a first grade teacher, signaling that it's time to come to the meeting rug in a corner of the classroom. There is a rush of activity as children scurry to put away coats, lunchboxes, papers, and pencils and make their way to the meeting rug. In less than a minute, twenty-five energetic first graders are funneling into the meeting area through two narrow passageways. Josiah and Theresa accidentally collide while trying to pass through an opening between two bookshelves. Theresa gives Josiah's shoulder a quick nudge and makes her way through. As she does, Josiah gives her an equally quick push from behind. Theresa falls forward, landing on three children who angrily begin yelling at her and complaining about squished fingers, hands, and knees. Theresa is fuming, Josiah sneering, while Ms. Ross untangles bodies and tries to restore order. By the time the group is finally settled and the Morning Meeting begins, the class is restless and the air heavy with tension.*

With twenty to thirty children sharing a classroom, there is always the possibility of minor bumps and collisions. While these mishaps can happen, a good design, especially in heavily used areas such as the whole-group meeting space, can greatly minimize their potential.

In the example above, it was a simple flaw in design that caused the collision, leading to confusion and chaos, and taking away valuable time from learning. Had there been three passageways into this meeting area instead of two, or had the passageways been wide enough for two children to easily fit through, the transition would have been a smooth one and the meeting that followed far more productive. Ms. Ross would have focused her energy on teaching rather than untangling, and the students would have come to the meeting rug feeling calm and ready to learn.

The Heart of the Classroom

The Heart
of the
Classroom

Where
Children Sit

The whole-group meeting area is of central importance in the classroom. It's the one place where the entire class can sit together in a circle and meet face-to-face. Sitting in a circle, everyone can see and be seen by everyone else. And because the circle has no beginning and no end, it allows everyone to hold an equal place in the group. By the very nature of its design, the meeting area invites group participation and fosters inclusion. Its presence and prominence in the classroom says to students, "In this classroom, we value working together and we value each individual's contributions to the group."

In many classrooms, students and teachers gather each morning in the meeting area to begin the day. Using a ritual called Morning Meeting, they come together in a circle to greet one another, share news, practice academic and social skills, and look forward to the events of the day ahead. This daily half-hour meeting sets a positive tone for the day, builds a sense of belonging and trust, and increases students' confidence and investment in their learning (see *The Morning Meeting Book* by Roxann Kriete for a thorough description).

The whole-group meeting area is also used widely for large-group and small-group problem-solving meetings; whole-group planning meetings; physical games and activities; conflict resolution; partner and small-group activities; and a broad range of instructional purposes.

In short, the whole-group meeting area is the heart of the learning environment, the place where the learning community is built and nourished.

Where Children Sit Makes a Difference in What They Learn

There are many benefits to having students sit in a circle for the majority of direct instruction. Whether introducing a new math concept or discussing a piece of literature, this seating arrangement sends an implicit but powerful message that "we are in a circle together for this lesson because your participation and contributions are critical to the success of this learning!"

Having students sit in a circle—as opposed to at desks and tables throughout the room or in rows like an "audience" in the meeting area—greatly increases student participation and investment. Here are some reasons why:

- *It minimizes the number of distractions.* When students sit at desks, they are often distracted by the desk's contents: pencils, papers, erasers, and various other personal belongings. Away from these distractions, their participation and attention greatly improve.

- *It allows the teacher to make direct eye contact with every child.* Making direct eye contact increases children's engagement, thus increasing their participation. It also allows the teacher to see students' facial expressions and gauge whether to adjust the content and pacing of the teaching.

- *It reduces potential "hot spots."* There's much research indicating that where students sit in a classroom affects their participation and the amount of attention they receive from the teacher. When students are seated at desks or tables throughout the classroom, teachers have tremendous difficulty including all students equally in whole-class instruction. Based on where the teacher stands, and regardless of student behavior, there are certain hot spots in the room that predictably draw a teacher's attention. When students are seated in a circle in the meeting area, on the other hand, it is easier for the teacher to attend to all students equally and elicit greater participation, which ultimately results in greater learning.

- *It creates a sense of intimacy and belonging, which helps children feel comfortable enough to take risks.* Children, like all of us, have a basic need to feel that they belong and have meaningful connections to the people around them. A whole-group meeting area can help. Here students can speak to each other without barriers. They can learn from and about each other in a familiar and intimate setting. In the safety of feeling included, known, and respected, they are more able to share their ideas, confront their struggles, and take the risks that learning requires.

The Whole-Group Meeting Area: A Flexible Space

The whole-group meeting area is a highly versatile area. The following photographs illustrate just a handful of ways that K–6 teachers and students use this space throughout the day.

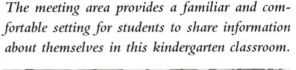

The meeting area provides a familiar and comfortable setting for students to share information about themselves in this kindergarten classroom.

Students and teachers gather for a Morning Meeting in a first grade classroom.

A whole-group geography lesson takes place in the meeting area in this third grade classroom.

Sixth graders gather in a circle for a problem-solving class meeting on the recent surge of teasing in the classroom.

The design of the area, with its rug and wide-open space, makes it welcoming for impromptu gatherings.

The meeting area provides a comfortable place for activities or games that require spreading out.

Third grade students gather in the meeting area to read the daily message board with news and announcements about the day ahead.

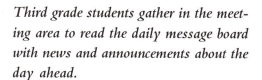

The meeting area is an ideal spot for active indoor activities, as shown in this first grade classroom.

Goals of Setting Up a Whole-Group Meeting Area

Because of its central role and significance in the classroom, the whole-group meeting area should be designed with the utmost care and attention. Essentially, a well-designed meeting area will:

- **Be inviting, spacious, and well defined**

- **Allow everyone to sit comfortably in a circle**

- **Allow everyone to make eye contact with everyone else**

- **Have entry pathways that allow for smooth, quick, and safe movement**

- **Allow for displays that are at or below children's eye level**

- **Be free of distractions and clutter**

Goals

Choosing a Good Site

GETTING STARTED

So, how do you create a meeting area that is inviting, well organized, and versatile? The first step is to choose a good site. Depending on the size and shape of the room, this step can range from being very simple to very challenging.

Choosing a Good Site

Below are some guidelines for selecting a site. The illustrations of floor plans on the following pages can also help you consider and map out possible locations.

- *The floor space should accommodate everyone comfortably in a circle.* There must be ample space for a true circle or oval and enough elbowroom for students to sit next to each other without touching. Giving students sufficient physical space will help them stay focused when they're in this area. There should be approximately three inches between each child and the next regardless of whether children are sitting on the floor, in chairs, or on a bench.

- *Select a space from which you'll have a clear view of the entire room, especially the room exits.* You need to be able to see anyone who might enter or leave the classroom, and to see what students are doing in other areas in the classroom. Knowing that you have a clear view of the classroom at all times helps students feel safe.

- *The space should not block pathways to room exits, bathrooms, closets, the sink area, or other heavily used areas.* Students should not have to walk over or through groups of children in the meeting space to get where they're going.

- *The space should be able to accommodate activities other than meetings.* While the primary function of the meeting area is to accommodate whole-group meetings and lessons, the space can and should be used for other purposes, as shown in the photographs on previous pages. I've seen countless possibilities for other uses: small-group lessons, drama activities, partner reading, math games, quiet activities, etc.

- *If possible, choose an area near a blackboard, a bulletin board, or other display space.* This allows you to showcase student work; display greetings, songs, and activities to use at Morning Meetings; post the calendar; and provide visual reminders of the rules and behavior expectations in the meeting area. Walls, bulletin boards, chalkboards, the tops and backs of shelving, and an easel pad (a display-sized pad of paper on a large easel) all provide suitable surfaces for displays.

- *Select an area that allows for good storage and easy access to an electrical outlet.* You need many tools and materials during meetings and lessons. The meeting area should allow for easy storage of an easel and easel pad, equipment for games and activities, a CD/tape player, and an overhead projector or video monitor if needed. (See Appendix B for a detailed description of the materials that might be needed in the meeting area and suggestions for purchasing and storing them.)

**Chapter
Three**

Meeting Area Site Plans

The diagrams below illustrate two possible locations for a whole-group meeting area. Use the space on the facing page to map out possible locations for the meeting area in your classroom.

Corner Meeting Area

Center Wall Meeting Area

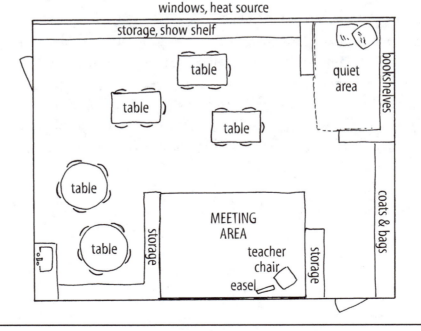

Use This Space to Plan Your Classroom

Where are the...?   Where do you want the...?

—doors   —meeting area

—windows   —work areas

—blackboards   —desks/tables

—heat sources   —storage/materials

**Chapter
Three**

Defining the Space

The more clearly defined the space is, with distinct boundaries and obvious pathways, the more successful students will be in coming to it and using it appropriately. There are many ways to physically delineate the meeting area, and many of them can be used together:

- *Use walls as boundaries.* Many teachers choose an area in front of a wall, in a corner where two walls come together, or at the end of a more narrow room bounded by three walls. Sites with walls as boundaries make excellent meeting areas. They are located away from much of the classroom traffic and often include a useful bulletin board or blackboard.

- *Use carpeting to identify the space.* A rug is a good option because its edges so clearly state the boundaries of the meeting space. In addition, it makes sitting on the floor more comfortable and lends the room a warm "homey" feeling, especially in a room with tile or wooden floors. (For more specific information on choosing a suitable rug, see Appendix B.) Carpet squares provide an inexpensive alternative. Most carpet stores will give carpet squares to teachers or sell them at a minimal cost. Low pile and colors that are bright but not too distracting work best. You can sew or tape the squares together so that they form a large rug.

- *Use furniture to establish boundaries.* A simple way to define the meeting area is to leave an open space and arrange furniture around it to create a boundary. The furniture might consist of clusters of desks, a table or two, several freestanding shelves, box benches (see description of these on the following page), or a combination of these. Most often teachers use furniture in conjunction with walls to create the space, but I have also seen successful designs in which the meeting area was set in the center of the room and the space was defined by the furniture circling it.

  Here are some specific suggestions about using furniture to define boundaries:

  Tables—Set tables back at least one-and-a-half to two feet from where students sit for their circle. This way, students sitting in chairs will be less likely to lean against the tables and those sitting on the floor will be less likely to sit under the tables and hit their heads.

  Desks—If the desks have an open end, face that end away from the meeting area. That way, children will not be distracted by objects in the desks.

Again, as with tables, place the desk clusters at least one-and-a-half to two feet from where students will sit for their circle.

Freestanding shelves—If the shelving has a back, turn that side toward the meeting area so it can be used for displays or back support for those sitting on the floor. Shelves should be low enough for the teacher to see over them when sitting in the meeting area. Also be sure shelves are stable enough to prevent tipping or sliding when children lean against or jostle them. Shelves with wheels usually have a brake that can be applied. To prevent sliding, you can use rubber floor protectors that go under shelf legs or rubber matting that can go under the entire shelf. Both are available in most hardware stores. If a shelf doesn't have a back, remember to organize the materials on it so that they will not create a distraction. Alternatively, use a curtain to cover the shelf during meetings and lessons when the materials are not in use.

Box benches—Low rectangular boxes, made from wood and covered with carpeting, make good seating for meetings (see illustration below). They can also be used to create a clear physical boundary for the meeting area. (For instructions on making box benches, see Appendix B.)

- **Mark the meeting spot with an easel pad.** For many teachers, an easel pad is an essential teaching tool for meetings and whole-class lessons. Teachers and students use it throughout the day. Students begin each morning by reading a message on the easel pad from their teacher welcoming them to school and highlighting something they'll be working on that day. The easel pad is then used throughout the day to record ideas and present information. In many classrooms, the easel pad is kept throughout the year as a running record of the class's daily activities. Central to all meetings, it can be used as the single piece of furniture or equipment that defines this space.

Establishing Pathways

In setting up the meeting area, think carefully about the pathways that lead in and out of it. Pathways should allow for smooth, quick, and safe movement. A few general guidelines regarding the width and number of pathways will help you prevent bottlenecks and other problems:

- Pathways should be wide enough for two children to walk comfortably past each other. When determining this width, think about all the possible uses of the space and the obstructions students might encounter when using the pathway. For example, if a pathway runs alongside a cluster of desks, then it must be wide enough to allow children to pass without disturbing those sitting at the desks. If a pathway runs past a supply shelf, the width of the pathway must also accommodate children standing at the shelf getting supplies.

Establishing
Pathways

Deciding
How Students
Will Sit

- The number of pathways needed depends on their width, the size of the classroom, the number of children in the class, and the age and development of the children. If the pathways are the minimum width recommended and the classroom size basically fits the number of children, there should be at least three pathways to the meeting area. If the pathways are more generous in width—wide enough for three or four children to walk side by side—and the size of the classroom basically fits the number of children, two pathways will generally be sufficient. If the number of students challenges the size of the room, it's likely that you'll need more pathways, wider pathways, and careful management during transitions.

Deciding How Students Will Sit

Will students sit on the floor? In chairs? On benches? Each option has distinct advantages and disadvantages as shown in the pros and cons chart on the following pages. In choosing seating, it's important to consider comfort, age appropriateness, and the need to be inclusive of all. Teachers of older students often involve the children in deciding how they will sit at the meeting area. Below are some things to consider for each option:

- *Sitting on the floor*—A rug or some kind of padded seating (individual rug squares or cushions) is essential to making this seating arrangement comfortable. Students can make simple pillows by decorating two pieces of oaktag, stapling them together, and stuffing them with newspaper. The softer the seating, the longer children will be able to sit and stay focused. If the rug is padded, most children will be able to sit comfortably through a group meeting or lesson, assuming that the length of the meeting or lesson is appropriate for the children's age.

Another way to make sitting on the floor more comfortable, especially for older students, is to provide some kind of back support. The simplest way to do this is to have students lean against a wall or the back of a shelf that forms a boundary for the meeting area. I have also seen various kinds of pillows, bean bags, and foam cushions work as back supports. I recently heard from a teacher whose parent teacher organization purchased for her class some of the portable backrests advertised in outdoor equipment or home furnishing catalogs.

- *Sitting on chairs*—The key here is to make sure the chairs are the right size. When sitting in the chair, a child's feet should rest flat on the floor. Having the right size chairs will help children feel comfortable and stay focused throughout a meeting.

- *Sitting on box benches*—These low rectangular boxes provide comfortable seating when covered with some sort of cushioning and built at an appropriate height. I've seen them used in all elementary grades. (For instructions on making box benches, see Appendix B.)

Another option that offers many of the benefits of the box benches but does not require construction is to use plastic milk crates (or their equivalent, now readily available in office and school supply stores). Flip the crates upside down and place a cushion on each. These seats can be easily stacked when not in use.

Deciding Where You Will Sit

Where teachers sit for meetings and whole-class lessons can play a critical role in the effectiveness of their teaching.

Ideally, you should:

- *Face the room exits and the rest of the room.* As mentioned earlier, children feel safer knowing their teacher can see the whole room. If your back is to the exits or the rest of the room, you won't be able to supervise the entire room.

- *Be where you can be closest to all the children.* Some meeting areas are only big enough to allow the class to sit in an oval shape rather than a true circle.

Seating Pros and Cons

	Pros	Cons
Sitting on the floor	▪ Children have space to spread out ▪ The informality encourages easy social interactions ▪ Feels natural for young children ▪ Allows quick transitions in and out of the meeting area	▪ Rug must be vacuumed and cleaned regularly ▪ Some children have difficulty respecting others' space (using individual rug squares can help) ▪ Children who can't sit on the floor (for example, children in wheelchairs) have to sit at a different level than their classmates ▪ Can be uncomfortable and cause restlessness
Sitting in chairs	▪ May be more comfortable, especially for older children ▪ Helps many children control their bodies and stay in their own space (typically not the case for five- and six-year-olds, who tend to have less control of their bodies when sitting in chairs) ▪ Provides back support and a clear physical boundary ▪ Often seen by children as a sign of maturity	▪ Generally requires a larger meeting area ▪ Requires children to learn and practice how to move chairs to and from the meeting area ▪ Transitions in and out of the meeting area take longer

Seating Pros and Cons

	Pros	Cons
Sitting on box benches	<ul><li>Allows quick transitions in and out of the meeting area</li><li>Often more comfortable than sitting on the floor</li><li>Children can rest clipboards for writing on their legs</li><li>Benches can be used in other parts of the room at other times</li></ul>	<ul><li>Benches cannot be purchased ready-made (however, they are simple to make, and high school shop classes are often willing to make them)</li><li>Benches need to be stacked and stored if not used outside of meeting times</li><li>Carpeting on the benches needs to be vacuumed and cleaned regularly</li></ul>

In this case it's important that you sit at the middle of the wide part of the oval. If you sit at a narrow tip, you'll be too far from the children at the other narrow tip.

- *Be near necessary teaching tools.* You should select a spot near the easel pad, blackboard, bulletin board, or area where materials for meetings or lessons are stored.

- *Take into consideration the developmental needs of the students.* In young primary grade (K–2) classrooms, for example, children depend on the consistency of classroom routines and classroom organization to feel safe. It's very important, therefore, that you sit in a consistent place for meetings and lessons if you teach at these grades. If you don't need to be near the easel pad or other teaching tools during a meeting and want to sit somewhere else, it's best to wait until the circle has formed before making the move.

Creating a Display Area

Many teachers find it essential to have space in the meeting area for displaying items that students will refer to when gathered there. These might include student work, calendars, rules, job charts, as well as greetings, songs, and activities to be used at Morning Meetings.

Walls, bulletin boards, chalkboards, the tops and backs of shelving, and the easel pad all provide suitable display surfaces. Below are some critical points to keep in mind when planning and designing meeting area displays. (For a more in-depth look at creating effective displays throughout the classroom, see Chapter Five, *Classroom Displays: A Tool for Teaching.*)

Creating a Display Area

- *Set displays at or below children's eye level.* Displays for children need to be accessible to children. Materials set above eye level are out of sight and therefore out of mind.

- *Keep displays visually simple and clear.* The old adage "less is more" is aptly applied here. To keep displays uncluttered, pare words and pictures so they convey only the most critical message, perhaps a brief synopsis of the essential information. In upper grades, children can participate in this process, practicing skills they have learned in direct instruction. In primary grades, teachers often demonstrate the process as a way of teaching it.

- *Display only what is most important.* In the meeting area, as in any area where display space is limited, it's essential to decide what is most important and to follow the "less is more" guideline. Make sure the displays have a function and support the goals of the meeting area, rather than just providing decoration.

Most meeting areas will have both permanent displays that convey critical information throughout the year and temporary displays that appear briefly or rotate in and out of the meeting area. Here are some examples of both kinds of displays:

Examples of Meeting Area Displays

- *A chart listing the names of everyone in the class, including the teacher*—This chart might also include photographs, especially at the young primary level when children are still learning to read each other's names. This display could be used to help with attendance, create partners and small working groups, designate jobs, etc.

- *A chart listing the specific behaviors that will support successful meetings and whole-class lessons*—Children and teachers usually establish these behavior guidelines together in a series of discussions and practice sessions. Often, everyone in the class signs this display, which serves as a frequent reminder during meetings and whole-class lessons.

- *A chart identifying the titles of greetings, activities, games, and songs that everyone in the group knows*—These can be used for Morning Meetings and stretching breaks during whole-class lessons. These lists grow throughout the school year.

- *The teacher's morning message to the children, written on the easel pad*— While this display changes every day, its content always speaks to the interests and academic work of the whole class. It also invites the children to interact with it in some way.

- *A creative, visual representation of the classroom community that everyone helps to make*—Some examples include a class name poster, a completed puzzle of names of all students in the class, or perhaps a "quilt" representing all class members.

- *A monthly calendar*—Many primary grade teachers use the calendar to teach math skills during Morning Meeting. Both the calendar and the related math activities can be displayed.

- *A job chart*—This can show students' classroom jobs for the day or for the week (see illustration).

- *A choice board*—This lists a variety of academic activities and the areas in the classroom where students can do the activities. By attaching their names to the choice board, children show what they will do when it is time for their choice work.

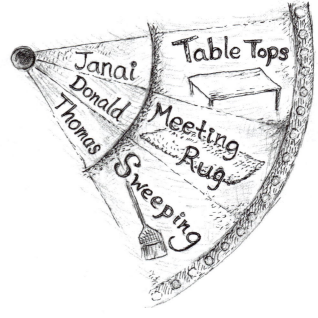

- *A sign-up sheet for Morning Meeting sharing*— Children who wish to share at the daily meeting can write their names on the sheet. Or the sign-up can be included as part of the teacher's daily written message on the easel pad.

A Sampling of
Meeting Area Displays

*Meeting Guidelines—
6th Grade*

Community Puzzle—4th Grade

*Word of
the Day—
2nd Grade*

Monthly Calendar—Kindergarten

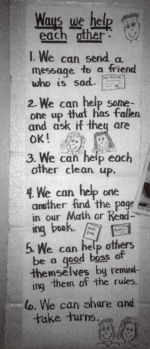

Ways We Help—
1st Grade

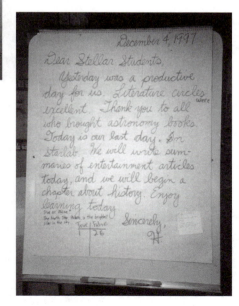

The Morning Message—
1st Grade

Classroom Rules—K/1

What's So Great?—1st Grade

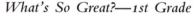

The Morning Message—5th Grade

FINE TUNINGS

Q. *I have 30 students, 30 desks, and a small room. There is no place to set up a permanent meeting area. What can I do?*

A. Unfortunately, this is not an unusual dilemma for teachers, especially in the intermediate grades, where class size is often pushed to the limit. A solution that has worked in many overcrowded classrooms is to create a temporary meeting area.

Whenever a meeting area is needed, the children move desks and other furniture to open up a large space for a circle. When the meeting is over, the students return the furniture to its original place. As you can imagine, this involves careful planning, skillful execution, and time. However, with adequate teaching and practice, children can set up and take down the meeting area in just a few minutes.

There are three important considerations in setting up a temporary meeting area:

First: How much furniture has to be moved and how hard is it to move? The site for a temporary meeting area should have as little furniture as possible and only pieces that students can easily move.

Second: What props will define the area and carry the message, "This is the place where we all come together, feel valued, and do meaningful work"? In classrooms with temporary meeting spaces, the easel pad typically becomes the symbol for the meeting area. Ideally, the easel pad would stay put and could serve as the point from which the meeting circle grows.

Third: How will you avoid a chaotic transition? Teaching and practicing how to move the furniture carefully, cooperatively, and quickly is the most critical factor in successfully creating temporary meeting spaces. Many teachers turn the practice into a game, such as trying to "Beat the Clock," to make the work fun. When teachers take the time to plan, teach, and practice the process step-by-step with their students at the beginning of the year, it can work smoothly and efficiently.

Q. *Bringing students together on the rug seems to provoke a number of problem behaviors, in particular, excessive wiggling, poking, not listening to or looking at the speaker, constantly moving into the middle of the circle "to see," and so forth. What do you suggest?*

A. Start by observing the children in the meeting area. You may find that the

Fine Tunings

root of the problem comes back to one or more flaws in the physical setup of the circle. Ask yourself the following questions:

Does the circle resemble an amoeba more than a true circle? If it does, students may be hidden behind each other or behind pieces of furniture. Out of the teacher's sight and unable to make eye contact with many of their class-mates, students lose touch with the circle and their part in it. This problem often occurs if the meeting area is a temporary one, requiring furniture rearrangements for every gathering.

Solution: As the circle forms, make sure that all furniture is pushed back enough to allow the circle to be round. Move bookshelves and tables that interfere with the circle or with the way children sit.

Is the space for the circle too small? If children are crowded together and don't have elbowroom, they will be unable to manage their bodies for even the shortest time. This is an especially common problem in temporary meeting areas.

Solution: Make sure the furniture is moved out far enough to allow a spa-cious circle. If using a rug, make sure its size is adequate. If it's too small, you can enlarge it by adding carpet squares to the sides. Young children benefit from having a prop that helps them know what size circle to make. Some teachers use tape or string to make a circle on the floor or on a rug. Others use tape to make an "X" to mark each seat in the circle.

Is there enough back support for children sitting on the floor? Some children really need back support in order to sit on the floor. Others are just more comfortable with back support. If children wiggle, move, lie down, and seem generally distracted, they probably need more back support.

Solution: If the problem is affecting only one or two children in the class, you might devise a solution that would help those children but not make them feel conspicuous. For example, you could provide a number of pil-lows, with the understanding that the students who most need them could always use them, and that other children could occasionally choose to use the extras. Or you might choose to switch everyone to chairs or benches.

Are there distracting shelves facing the meeting area? Are they stacked with materials that are interesting and invite touching?

Solution: Some children need all the support they can get in controlling their impulses, including a meeting area that is as free from distraction and temptation as possible. Organize meeting area shelves with a few materials that fit well. Remove materials that particularly invite touching, or cover them with a lid or shelf curtain.

Q. *Many of my students argue over where to sit when they come to the meeting area. We sit on a rug and they argue over who gets to be by the wall and who gets to have the pillows in the corner. What do you suggest?*

A. First, consider the comfort factor. Perhaps the wall and pillows provide back support and are therefore more comfortable. Discuss the issue with the children. Perhaps they'll choose to rearrange the meeting area so they'll have more back support or so they can sit in chairs. Or they may devise a fair way to take turns using the wall and the pillows.

Fine Tunings   Another possibility is to combine various forms of seating: wall support, shelf support, pillow support, and benches. This option offers more flexibility in the design of the meeting area and gives students a variety of seating options. To avoid the arguments over where students will sit, teachers who use this approach spend time teaching children how to take turns with the various options.

Q. *I have a limited classroom budget and cannot afford to purchase an easel stand and pad. Is the blackboard adequate for writing messages and recording notes from meetings?*

A. While I feel the easel pad is ideal for these purposes, it is certainly not the only tool that will work. Blackboards and dry-erase boards can work, though the disadvantage is that the information on them often gets erased inadvertently, and the information can't be saved throughout the year. Also, a permanent wall blackboard is often not at the right height for all children to read from or reach to for writing. Some teachers solve these problems by pinning or taping a single sheet of paper to a bulletin board, blackboard, or wall so that it hangs at the right height for children.

Another alternative to using an easel is to purchase an inexpensive piece of Masonite or bulletin board. Attach paper to it, and place this "pad" on a painting easel or a small inexpensive tripod chart holder. You could even place the pad on a stool, chair, shelf, or small tabletop to give it height and then lean it against a wall, shelf, or chair back for stability.

Q. *I use an easel pad, but I worry increasingly about the overuse of paper in our environment. It seems like such a waste. What do you think?*

A. Although this is an important point, I believe easel pad paper can be used wisely. Many conscientious teachers use both sides of the paper and keep the pads for the year, making the contents available to the children as a visual history of their class and their year of learning together. Over and over I see children referring to information located on an easel pad page or practicing their emerging reading skills as they pore over the contents of an easel pad. Some teachers send the easel pad pages home with individual children as a way of helping them share more about school at home.

Q. *I have heard that the teacher should model "being an equal member of the community" by sitting exactly as the children sit. If the children sit on the floor, the teacher should sit on the floor. I feel guilty when I sit in an adult-sized chair at circle time, but my knees no longer allow me to easily sit on the floor. What are your thoughts on this?*

A. Teachers' bodies, like children's bodies, come in all sizes and shapes and therefore have different needs. The floor may no longer be practical for some pairs of knees. And some teachers just don't fit in small first grade chairs!

While I support the goal and philosophy of the teacher sitting on the same level and in the same way as the children as much as possible, I also believe that the teacher's seating should provide what is necessary for the teacher to work comfortably.

The details of how we arrange the physical environment do influence our work, but our relationships and interactions with children have an even greater impact. A teacher who treats children with respect and kindness and demonstrates through daily words and actions that s/he values every student's contribution won't be considered arrogant, authoritarian, or self-centered simply because s/he sits in an adult-sized chair. Offered an explanation, children will likely accept that a teacher needs a chair of a different size to be comfortable.

All that said, I do believe that the kind of chair we choose to sit in at the meeting area does make a difference in the message we send to children. A teacher who sits in a simple, adult-sized straight-back chair similar to the children's sends a different message than the teacher who sits in an oversized, padded office chair or a large stuffed armchair that dominates the circle. Children are deeply aware of these messages, so it's important to consider them when setting up a classroom.

Chapter Four

FURNITURE, MATERIALS, AND STORAGE: SETTING UP FOR CURRICULUM

W*hat makes a hiccup start?*
How do muscles make bones move?
What happens to food in your body?
Why does cold make you shiver?

These questions, among others generated by students about the human body, hang prominently in the meeting area where twenty-five fourth graders gather excitedly to begin a science work period.

Each student has chosen one area of the body to study. Some do research on the nervous system, others the digestive system. A small group studying the muscular system is engrossed in planning experiments on the reflexes while another group gathers materials for a papier-mâché and wire model of the skeletal system. Students work on the computer, in the class library, in the hallway rehearsing a skit, and on the phone conducting interviews with local doctors. The room is alive, humming with the energy of purposeful activity.

Two children studying the circulatory system use clear plastic tubing and a pump from a science kit to make a model of how blood flows through the body. After several failed attempts to make the water flow through the tubes, the teacher suggests they bring the problem to the whole class for help.

With ten minutes left in the period, Mr. G. calls the children back to the meeting area for reflection. *What went well today? Who has some discoveries to share?* David describes four new facts about the digestive system. Sasha and Emma share that they've finally completed their list of all the bones in the body. Mr. G. asks, *Anything hard about today's work? Does anyone have a problem or question they'd like to bring to the group?* The two students working on the blood flow model share their difficulties and ask for suggestions. Finally, everyone takes a few minutes to write down reflections, results, and plans for the following day.

Children learn best in an environment where the learning is active and inquiry-based. In the example above, the curriculum is not something that is handed down to children. Instead, children are active participants, with the content of the curriculum growing at least in part from their own interests and questions.

These students have many choices in their learning, choices about what they'll study, who they will work with, where they'll work, what materials they will use, and how they'll represent what they've learned. Many styles of learning are honored and students are encouraged and taught how to work together and learn from each other.

By structuring activities that demand initiative and risk-taking, the teacher encourages students to think independently, to plan and try out their ideas, to reflect on their mistakes, and to try again. By structuring activities that require group and partner work, the teacher encourages cooperative learning and gives children plenty of opportunities to practice the social skills necessary to work collaboratively.

For a curriculum rich with active learning opportunities to work well, the physical arrangement of the classroom must support it. Whether you're teaching math, reading, art, or science, the physical setup of the classroom will have a significant impact on your instruction. Designed poorly, the setup will stand in the way of your teaching; designed thoughtfully, it will make your best teaching possible.

Goals of Setting Up for Curriculum

Goals of Setting Up for Curriculum

A classroom set up for active learning allows considerable flexibility. It allows students to work in small groups, in large groups, with a partner, and independently. It accommodates a variety of teaching methods, and it provides for both student-initiated and teacher-initiated learning experiences. Specifically, this means:

- **Furniture that allows the greatest amount of flexibility and a wide range of instructional approaches and student work styles**

- **Materials that are varied, accessible, age-appropriate, and in good working condition**

- **Storage that is well defined and accommodates a wide variety of works in progress**

GETTING STARTED

**Chapter
Four**

Arranging the Furniture

While the reality of a classroom is that it's a finite space, try to imagine its uses to be as limitless and as varied as possible.

Plan for a variety of work places.

Ideas for creating work places that are private and quiet:

- Assign seats at a table for writing time.

- Set up work stations. These can be individual desks set apart in the room for solitary work.

- Designate a comfortable "quiet place" in the classroom that children may use one at a time just to be alone.

Ideas for creating work places that encourage cooperation and collaboration:

- Set up a permanent space large enough to hold the whole class for spontaneous and planned whole-class and small-group meetings.

- Put several round tables in different parts of the room for small-group instruction or small-group projects.

- Group desks together in clusters.

- Provide space and materials in a block-building area to allow six to eight children to work there at one time.

- Store math, language arts, and strategy games beside a comfortable rug or a desk cluster to encourage children to work in small groups.

- Set up computer stations that allow partners to work together.

Arranging the Furniture

Ideas for offering a variety of work surfaces and accommodating a variety of work styles:

- Create a large space where children can spread out and stretch their legs or work on murals, maps, and other large art projects.

- Provide straight-backed chairs, one or two rockers, some pillows or an armchair, and perhaps box benches, so children can find a place and way to work that's comfortable for them.

- Have a place where children can work listening to quiet music on earphones.

- Provide clipboards and "workboards" (1/4" Masonite, 12" x 18"–24" x 24") for work that can be taken anywhere.

Ideas for creating cozy spaces for reading, writing, or resting:

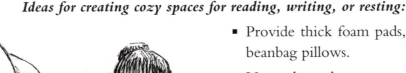

- Provide thick foam pads, throw pillows, or beanbag pillows.

- Use a large box to create a small "hut." Simply reinforce the corners with clear strapping tape, cut out a doorway and windows, and decorate the box with paint or contact paper.

- Get one of the many small, easy-to-assemble "pup" tents on the market today to set up and take down in the room as desired.

Plan for the greatest possible flexibility.

Many teachers, with the good intention of providing a rich and varied environment, over-fill their classrooms with a wide assortment of furniture and materials. While this may provide a variety of work places, it also makes the room feel crowded. Better to have less furniture and material that can be used in multiple ways.

Providing for the greatest amount of flexibility in the classroom can be a daunting task. Here are two rules that might help:

> *Rule #1: All children should be able to sit upright in front of a flat work surface at any given time. Seating might be a straight-backed chair, stool, or bench, and the work surface might be a desk, table, or pullout shelf.*

> *Rule #2: Most of the workspaces and furniture should allow more than one use within a school day or in the course of the school year as the curriculum and the needs of the students change. Carefully scrutinize any space or furniture that does not allow multiple uses.*

Chapter Four

Here are a few concrete examples to illustrate this concept of flexibility:

- In a sixth grade classroom, four to six desks clustered together provide individual assigned workspaces for children during language arts time. During math time, the same desks become a space for two to six children to play one of the math games stored on a nearby shelf. Laying a thin sheet of Masonite over the desks, a small group of students use the space to create a timeline during history.

- In the beginning of the year in a second grade classroom, the desks are arranged in pairs because seven-year-olds are more comfortable working alone or in pairs than in large groups. As the year progresses and students become more skilled in working and socializing in larger groups, the teacher arranges groups of four and then six desks, thus extending the possibilities for their use.

- In a fourth grade classroom, a rectangular table is set near a science bulletin board and used for several weeks to carry out and display electricity experiments with batteries and bulbs. Initially, the teacher uses the table to instruct a small group of children and to store materials. An adjacent bulletin board provides a place to display the initial hypotheses and findings, the weekly and daily challenges, and the experiment results. Once the students know how to use the materials, the teacher stores the materials on stacked shelves on a small desk below the bulletin board. The children are then able to take the materials they need and work in other parts of the room. The large table is moved to a spot near the sink, where it becomes a work table for a group of students completing a mural of the Westward Expansion.

Mix furniture used for seating, material storage, and displays.

Instead of putting all the students' desks in the middle of the room and all the supply shelves and displays on the periphery, it's best to intersperse the materials and displays among the desks whenever possible. The message implicit in this design is that student-initiated learning, access to a wide array of materials, and student choice are important and valued.

Arranging the Furniture

Leave no space wasted or unused.

As you place each piece of furniture, stand back and see if you've met the guidelines for variety and flexibility of use. Then take a second hard look to see if you've created any "dead spaces" or partially unused spaces in the room.

One place I often see wasted space is around the teacher's desk. In placing the desk so that it faces the children, teachers often leave a large amount of space behind the desk so they can get to the chair. The irony is that teachers rarely sit at their desks during the school day when the children are present. If you simply turn the desk around and place its front against a wall, the desk and chair will take up a lot less space.

Other potential dead spaces to be aware of are:

- Areas near room exits and closets
- Spaces behind bookcases and room dividers
- Corners of the room or any corners created by furniture
- Spaces around classroom computers
- Spaces under and next to wall blackboards

Finally, the ultimate "dead space" is the area above all the furniture that reaches up to the ceiling. In most cases, however, that space is not wasted at all. This open space is, in fact, absolutely necessary because it provides children and teachers not only with headroom to move about, but also with an unobstructed visual field providing light, clarity, and space. In most classrooms, the open, uncluttered use of this area is critical to creating a sense of spaciousness.

Choosing Materials

Although we all might wish to have a limitless supply of classroom learning materials, our space will not allow it, even if our school budgets will. However, it's possible to stock our classrooms with an assortment of learning materials without overcrowding the learning environment.

Make sure materials really work.

If children are to do quality work, they must have quality tools. When children are engaged and invested in their learning and taught how to care for materials, supplies can last a long time. And in many cases, quality materials will outlast cheap ones, reducing overall purchasing in the long run. Below are some qualities to look for in common classroom materials:

- *Scissors* should be sharp and able to cut anything from cloth to cardboard. Quality scissors can serve a classroom for many years as long as they have an occasional sharpening.

- *Glue* containers should have a top that opens easily and prevents the glue from clogging and drying out. Liquid glue should flow well without being "runny." Glue in stick form should be non-wrinkle and clear-drying. Rubber cement should be non-toxic and easily rubbed off.

- *Markers* should be in brilliant colors with various sized tips and generously flowing ink. Markers should also be available in multi-ethnic skin tones. The ink should not dry out quickly as long as the markers are properly cared for.

- *Crayons and colored pencils* should offer an inspiring array of colors, including a wide variety of skin colors.

- *Clay* should be available in a variety of colors, including diverse skin tones, and shouldn't leave a greasy film on hands.

Choose materials with multiple uses.

A classroom that pulses with the excitement of learning is one that offers children a wide variety of experiences. Along with reading, writing, and math, there should be music, dance and movement, the visual arts, handcrafts, drama, cooking, outdoor exploration, field trips, use of computer technology, and more. The materials in the classroom need to encourage children to be creative, use their senses, ask questions, do hands-on exploration, and learn in as many ways as possible.

Choosing Materials

By providing materials that can be used in a variety of ways, a teacher can ensure this wide array of possibilities without overloading the classroom shelves. Examples of materials that can have many uses include:

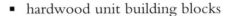

- hardwood unit building blocks
- Legos in younger grades
- math manipulatives
- art materials for model building, painting, collage, and drawing
- writing materials
- a variety of drama props and costumes
- science tools, such as magnifying glasses, tweezers, probes, eye droppers, Q-tips, measuring devices, balances, weights, pulleys, and magnets
- recycled materials

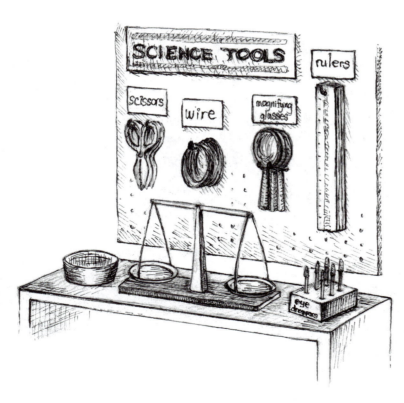

Provide materials to help children plan and reflect on their learning.

This is an important way to promote autonomy and initiative. Here are a few suggestions:

- *Post a daily schedule in a central location.* (For younger students, it's enough to list the sequence of events without the times.) Children need to be aware of the schedule to do their best planning. You can write the schedule on a blackboard, post it on the chart stand, or use a "sentence strip" chart. The key is to put the schedule where the whole class can see it—and to go over it every day, if only to acknowledge that everyone has read it.

- *Set up a planning board where children can record which activities they've chosen to do.* Whether you designate one period each day when children may choose their work or let children decide for themselves when to do choice work, a planning board is an effective way for children to identify their decisions. (See Appendix B for suggestions for making a planning board.)

- *Provide materials for children to write their work plans for the day or for a particular subject.* Many teachers provide children with daily planning worksheets. Others, particularly in the upper grades, provide notebooks in which children develop their own method of recording their plans. These materials allow children to maintain an ongoing record of their work and support them as they practice organizing and taking responsibility for their work and learning.

Chapter Four

- *Have a place for children to sign up to share their work.* Children should be encouraged to share the process and outcomes of their work. Some teachers like to use the end of the day for sharing to reinforce a sense of community just before students leave. Others prefer to share immediately following a long period of work that involved many children. Whichever the case, students may be more engaged in the process if they sign up and take steps to prepare for their sharing. The signup can be as simple as a sheet of paper, a small blackboard, or a spiral notebook. As with the planning board and daily schedule, it should be in a place that's accessible to all.

- *Provide materials to help children reflect on their work.* Daily reflection helps children develop self-awareness and become self-motivated learners. Teachers foster reflection by setting aside time for it, by ensuring that there are enough spaces in the classroom conducive to it, and by frequently asking questions such as *What worked well today? What didn't work? What was hard?* and *What was interesting?* Many teachers provide students with reflection worksheets that accompany planning worksheets or ask students to answer reflection questions in the same notebooks they use for planning.

Choose materials that reflect students' cultural and ethnic backgrounds.

Children will feel more invested in the curriculum and have a stronger sense of belonging if classroom materials reflect their various cultural and ethnic backgrounds. In addition, classroom materials should celebrate the diversity of our whole world. Whenever possible, teachers should seek out multicultural materials, such as multiracial dolls and literature that represents a wide variety of cultural and ethnic backgrounds.

Choose materials that promote understanding of people who face physical and cognitive challenges.

Choosing Materials

Teachers have a responsibility to help children develop an understanding of people's differences and challenges. Whenever possible, teachers should include materials that reflect the lives and experiences of people who are physically and cognitively challenged. For example, primary grade teachers can include dolls and props for drama and social studies that expose children to the experiences of being physically challenged. Teachers of all grades can select literature that reflects the experiences of those who are physically and cognitively challenged.

Make sure materials reflect a range of interests and ability levels.

Classroom materials should meet the needs of all learners. So there's something for everyone, reading materials should range widely in difficulty level and content, and include everything from comic books to nonfiction magazines. Most classrooms also have math and language games that are suitable for children with a wide range of skills and interests. For example, the math and language games in a third grade classroom might include Pick-up Sticks, cards, Lotto, Scrabble, checkers, and chess. (See Appendix A for specific material suggestions.)

Consider children's age and development when choosing materials.

As discussed in Chapter One, in choosing classroom materials and equipment, it's important to understand the developmental skills of the children. For example, consider a first grade classroom:

Most six-year-olds are just beginning to be able to think logically, understand cause and effect, and conserve number and volume. They benefit greatly from materials such as unit building blocks, math manipulatives, and a sand and water table to test their growing understanding of numbers, volume, and measurement.

Six-year-olds are also developing an increased understanding of the difference between fantasy and reality. They need opportunities to dramatize their understanding of how things work in the real world. Props and costumes that allow them to act out the themes they're learning about in social studies would therefore be appropriate.

Appendix A offers checklists of materials generally appropriate for children in grades K–6.

Chapter Four

Storing Materials

An obvious purpose of storage is to protect materials and keep them from obstructing work in the classroom. However, storage also should display materials in a way that makes them inviting and accessible to learners. Proper storage can highlight materials and extend the possibilities for in-depth learning.

Use a variety of storage shelves.

One size does not fit all when it comes to shelves. For example, if shelves are too narrow, materials will stick out and get knocked off. If shelves are too wide, they will quickly become overcrowded, and materials will likely be overlooked and unused. Here are some general guidelines for storage shelves:

- Wide shelves work well for globes, balances, and other large science and math materials. These should sit at children's eye level. One simple way to create a wide top shelf for these materials is to put two bookcases back to back. Another way is to place a wide board on top of a bookcase.

- Wide shelves are necessary for the large bins used to store sets of math manipulatives, sets of games that go together, and recycled materials.

- Standing files placed on the floor or on a wide shelf can be used to store student work folders. Be sure nothing goes above children's eye level.

- Narrow shelves work best for smaller writing tools, art materials, and for smaller game boxes. (Hanging shoe pockets can be used for the same purpose.)

- In primary classrooms, a variety of wide and narrow shelves is necessary for storing hardwood unit building blocks. Because these blocks are heavy and used primarily on the floor, it's important to store them on shelves low to the ground. It's also critical to store them in classified order rather than all together in bins or haphazardly on shelves. By stacking blocks with like units in their designated spot on a shelf, children learn classification skills and develop a deeper appreciation for the material.

Storing Materials

Not many teachers have the luxury of being able to buy shelving whenever they need it. Here are two suggestions for creating reasonably priced shelving that works well.

Quick and Easy Shelving

- *Place a wooden plank over two plastic milk crates or two painted cement blocks.* If you want several layers, place something with weight into the crates to make the shelves sturdy. If the bookshelf is higher than two layers, place it against a wall or another bookshelf.

- *Simply stack plastic milk crates one on top of the other or side by side to create a series of open cubicles for storage.* To increase the sturdiness, strap the crates together with velcro strips.

Finally, fold-up hardwood bookshelves, available in most all-purpose stores, are a good choice for classroom storage. While these cost more than other shelving options, they have definite benefits: they're collapsible, making them easy to store when not in use; they're spacious and sturdy, yet light enough to be transported easily; and, if you are paying for the bookshelf out of pocket, they're suitable for home-use should you no longer need them in the classroom.

Provide places to store ongoing projects.

Ongoing projects may include large flat posters and murals, three-dimensional projects of varying sizes, art work that needs to dry before being stacked, and projects involving special materials such as drama props, musical instruments, or even carpentry tools. Here are a few ideas for storing works in progress:

- Allocate wall space and hang work using mounting putty (available in most hardware or office supply stores). The space can be above eye level, since the work is not intended for full display yet.

- Set aside part of a bookcase or shelf. In order to define the space and protect the work, use a low-sided plastic container to hold the work. The container can be stabilized with mounting putty, weather strip, or caulking cord.

- Run a piece of rope along the front of a wall for hanging work. (Avoid running a rope from one corner of the room to another, as that clutters the visual field.)

- Use several portable, collapsible laundry racks for hanging work. Keep a container of clothespins nearby.

- Create narrow spaces for stacking flat work that needs to dry by placing cardboard or thin sheets of Masonite on small blocks of wood.

- Attach pegboard to a wall or the back of a bookcase. In pairs, set 2"-long pegs in the board at a specific horizontal distance apart. Put holes at the same distance apart in paper that needs to hang. The long pegs allow several pieces of work to hang one behind the other.

- Use skirt hangers to hang pieces of work one behind the other. The skirt hangers can hang from a coat rack in a closet, a hanging chart stand, or a rope strung across a wall.

- Use a tall plastic wastebasket for storing work that can be rolled up. Be sure to label it well so children will see that it is not to be used as a wastebasket. Keep a container of rubber bands nearby.

- Keep handy a few plastic boxes with lids or milk crate containers to store play props, carpentry tools, etc.

Whatever storage spaces you create, be sure to label them clearly as space for works in progress. Also pay careful attention to keeping these areas neat and organized. When not deliberately taken care of, projects can often be destroyed before they are even completed. Finally, make sure children get in the habit of putting their names on their work. It helps to hang a pencil with string at each storage place.

Chapter Four

FINE TUNINGS

Q. *I would like to create a writing area in my classroom where all the writing materials will be easily accessible and the atmosphere will be quiet and conducive to writing, but I just don't have the space. What alternatives should I consider?*

Fine Tunings

A. While many teachers like to devote a part of their classroom to writing and storing writing materials, this in fact can be a limiting way of using precious space. Instead of giving children just one place to write, encourage children to look at the entire classroom for possible spots. During a writing time, make all the empty tables and unused desks available. If you provide clipboards or Masonite "workboards," children can have instant portable writing surfaces and can use floor space and other nooks for writing. As a result, every child can choose where to write, and the classroom space and furniture get more flexible use. Finally, storing writing materials separate from other similar learning tools can take up a lot of space. I suggest keeping unusual or special writing materials with the art supplies, and the more general writing tools on top of tables or desks where children have easy access to them.

Q. *Lately there has been a movement to encourage teachers to remove their own desks from the classroom. I realize my desk takes up a fair amount of space and that I rarely sit at it, but I can't imagine how I would organize my materials and manage my paperwork without it. What are your thoughts on this?*

A. Every teacher needs private space in the classroom. This space is critical to the teacher's ability to be organized, focused, and effective. For the children, the very presence of this space teaches and affirms the right of all individuals, including teachers, to have social and physical boundaries that give privacy.

Therefore, the question is not whether a teacher should have private work and storage space, but how much space should be allotted. Given the space limitations in most classrooms, I suggest that teachers limit their furniture to a few essential pieces that take up minimal space and serve multiple uses whenever possible.

If you are considering removing your desk but need a place to store materials and papers, you may want to keep a file cabinet and a few bookshelves deep enough to hold plastic bins and letter trays for your private use. In addition, some teachers keep a small desk for their own use. This could be a student desk, a small "home type" desk, or even a makeshift desk made by placing a small, rectangular piece of plywood (Birch plywood works well) or Formica across the top of two file cabinets. If you do use plywood, give it several coats of polyurethane in order to create a smooth, hard surface for writing.

Q. *I would like to buy quality materials for my classroom, but our school requires that all purchases be made through a bidding process. If I ask the children to bring in their own supplies, some will bring in much better quality materials than others. What can I do about this?*

A. Unfortunately, tight budgets force many schools to bid for materials, and classrooms often end up with very low quality supplies. If families purchase their own children's supplies, the resulting inequality and division within the classroom may be hurtful, just as you suggest. Here are some ways that teachers address these problems, aside from purchasing quality materials out of their own pockets:

Chapter Four

- Go to the parent organization and request funds to purchase quality materials for the classroom. Explain how the materials will be used and the advantages of purchasing higher quality tools.

- Discuss the issue of poor quality materials with the class and let the students take on the problem. Some classes have decided to run fundraisers to purchase supplies for school.

- In some schools where it's standard practice for parents to provide their children's supplies, teachers can approach the issue in two ways:

    1. Give families a list of quality materials to purchase, specifying brand names when appropriate. Make it clear that the materials are intended for the whole class. The teacher collects the materials, stores them, and brings them out as the children need them.
    2. Ask families to contribute a set amount of money, which is then pooled to purchase materials for use by the whole class.

Both approaches require sending a letter to families, explaining the policy change and the overall educational purpose. Before making a change like this, it's important to consult with your principal. The more support you have for the change and the more teachers who participate, the more likely it will be successful. No matter what you do, be sensitive to families who cannot afford to contribute, and make sure you have a plan that will not cause embarrassment to children with fewer resources.

Chapter Five

CLASSROOM DISPLAYS: A TOOL FOR TEACHING

Imagine being a small child walking into your classroom in September. Everywhere you look you see walls and bulletin boards decorated with shiny store-made or teacher-made displays. Perfect looking pictures and neatly printed signs fill the room with only a few spaces left empty for children's work. What are the messages? This room belongs to the teacher, your work will never measure up to what the teacher likes to have on display, and perhaps even worse, your interests don't matter here.

While I use an extreme example to illustrate a point, it's not uncommon to see classrooms where teacher-created or store-bought displays and decorations cover much of the space, making students feel like they've stepped into a party store rather than a classroom. The teacher's intention is probably to make the room welcoming and engaging by filling it with color and liveliness. However, the effect on children is often the opposite, making them feel overwhelmed and inconsequential.

Classroom displays that celebrate students' efforts and have a connection to the daily life of the classroom are one of the most powerful—and overlooked—tools for teaching. They can generate excitement about the curriculum, increase children's investment in learning, help children to appreciate their own work and the work of others, and foster a powerful sense of individual and group ownership of the classroom.

Creating displays such as these doesn't necessarily require endless hours of teacher time. In fact, while there will always be some displays the teacher creates completely on her/his own, the majority of the displays addressed in this chapter are ones created through a genuine collaboration among students and teachers.

Goals of Creating Classroom Displays

At their best, classroom displays:

- **Acknowledge and celebrate every child's efforts**

- **Build a sense of individual and group ownership of the classroom**

- **Have a meaningful connection to the curriculum, serving as an effective tool for teaching**

- **Generate excitement about learning**

Goals

Make Children's Work the Primary Focus

GETTING STARTED

Make Children's Work the Primary Focus of Classroom Displays

A classroom filled with the work of children is not only a delight to be in, but also sends the powerful message to students that their work and their learning are most important in this classroom. Here are some suggestions for making children's work the focal point of displays:

- *Keep store-bought displays to a minimum.*

- *Invite children to create posters and signs.* Children will learn more about the alphabet, phonics, and the rules of grammar if they are involved in making these posters rather than just reading ones bought from a store. Making the poster becomes part of learning the information. The poster itself becomes more meaningful because the children have invested their effort in its creation.

- *Create displays that honor effort and not just perfectly mastered work.* Displays should make every child feel valued regardless of his or her academic abilities. Whenever possible, avoid using grades, stickers, or marks on children's work, especially work that will be displayed.

- *Make sure that the efforts of every child are reflected in at least one display.* Some teachers have each student create a display square at the beginning of the year (see illustration). Each square has a photograph of the child and a name card decorated by the student. Placed throughout the classroom, these squares are used to display each child's work throughout the year.

    Another possibility is to always have one display that reflects the efforts of everyone in the class. These displays affirm each child's sense of belonging and have a powerful effect on creating community. (See examples of all-class displays on the following page.)

- *Create displays that reflect the class's identity as a community of learners.* There are many ways that teachers can use displays to affirm the class's sense of community and shared purpose. Here are a few examples:

    - *A display of the class rules or the class constitution beautifully written and signed by every student*

    - *A list of the students' and teacher's "Hopes and Dreams" for the school year*

    - *Lists of commonly known songs, activities, and Morning Meeting greetings*

    - *A display of class surveys or class achievements*

- *Use teacher displays selectively.* Teacher displays allow a teacher to provide information to children in a variety of formats. Teachers might want to display charts showing ideas from brainstorming sessions with the children, posters with pictures and information relevant to the curriculum, three-dimensional models (such as the human body, or the sun and moon in orbit), directions for various routines, or collections of nonfiction books. When creating teacher displays, remember to:

Samples of All-Class Displays

This second-grade "Pride Photo Poster" shows each child doing something that he or she feels proud of and has demonstrated to the class, such as riding a bike, playing the piano, or reading a book. This idea came from Bob Strachota, a teacher at Greenfield Center School.

Samples of All-Class Displays

These beginning-of-the-year handwriting samples are displayed in a fourth grade classroom.

First graders' "Hopes and Dreams" for the school year are displayed on bulletin boards in the hallway.

- *Display only what is immediately useful.* If you haven't used or referred to a display in the last two weeks, put it away and bring it out again when you need it. When there are too many displays, they lose their meaning.

- *Make sure information is relevant and useful to the children.* These displays should be appropriate to the age, development, and interests of the children and relevant to the curriculum. They should be tools for teaching and learning, not for celebrating a series of holidays, for example, with no meaningful connection to the curriculum. They should also meet the current needs of students. For example, many primary classrooms have a "word wall" to help children spell common words. This is a relevant and useful display when the words come directly from the children's current writing. (See Fine Tunings for a word of caution about word wall use.)

- *Heighten children's awareness of teacher displays that are posted in the classroom for the entire year.* There will always be some displays—such as the alphabet and numbers, cursive letter formation, phonics charts, and classroom rules—which teachers will want on display throughout the year. So that these displays don't simply fade into the background, let children participate in creating them or recreating them in their own writing and style.

Keep All Display Areas Simple and Uncluttered

Ideally, displays will reveal the life of the classroom with beauty, clarity, and simplicity. Here are some guidelines to help you achieve this:

- *Only display a few items at a time in any one area.* To avoid overwhelming the children, put up only what's necessary and most useful to them at any given time.
- *Change or rotate items rather than continually adding to them.* This keeps the children's interest high and allows for the work of many students to be represented.
- *Define each piece of work.* Label and frame children's work to draw attention to it. (Various options for framing and labeling work will be addressed later in the chapter.)
- *Use a plain color and texture for the background.* Remember the goal is to highlight the work, not the background! A solid color or a design with a small, quiet print works best.
- *Keep the visual field clear.* As you look across the room, you should be able to see every area without obstructions. Lacking wall space, many teachers choose to hang displays from the ceiling. Not only is this a fire hazard, but if the displays are hung at children's eye level, they obstruct the children's visual field. This creates a sense of clutter and disorganization, ultimately interfering with children's ability to do their best work. If the displays are hung high, then they are no longer in the children's natural viewing range.

Keep Display Areas Simple

Use Location to Maximize the Value

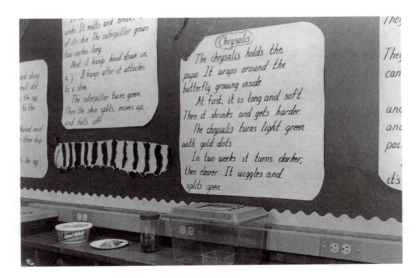

Use Location to Maximize the Value of Displays

Where displays are located makes an enormous difference in how well they're used. Here are some suggestions for making displays accessible and relevant:

- *Put the display near a relevant work area.* For example, if a display is intended to show the results of children's ongoing experiments with plants, then it should be located directly beside where those experiments are done. This strategic placement stimulates thinking, promotes an exchange of ideas, and provides a useful reference for students.

- *Locate displays so children can see them.* It's essential that displays be at children's eye level. If your classroom has bulletin boards or blackboards that are too high, you can try to lower the bulletin boards, place a sturdy step stool beside the high bulletin boards or blackboards, or create new display areas and use the existing bulletin board for another purpose. In areas where children often sit in chairs or on the floor, it may make sense to put some displays at a point lower than eye level.

- *Have bulletin boards throughout the classroom.* Better to have many bulletin boards throughout the room than one large one that's likely to get overcrowded. You can use any flat surface, including the back of a bookshelf, the side of a file cabinet, or the lower part of a wall or door, by attaching a bulletin board or cork material to it. I've seen many teachers use the front of their desks for children to sign up for lunch, to record daily attendance, or to hang their work. (See Fine Tunings for more ideas on making bulletin boards.)

- *Locate hanging displays along a wall or across a set of windows.* An alternative for classrooms short on wall space or bulletin boards is to stretch one or two laundry lines at eye level across a wall or across a set of windows and hang displays from them. This creates more display space without cluttering children's field of vision.

- *Find a good location for displaying items children bring in to share.* Children often bring in items to share that have special meaning to them. It's important to have a place to display these items that both protects them from damage and makes them easily accessible for viewing. A wide windowsill, top shelf, or low table, ideally located near the meeting area where the child will likely be sharing the item, can work well.

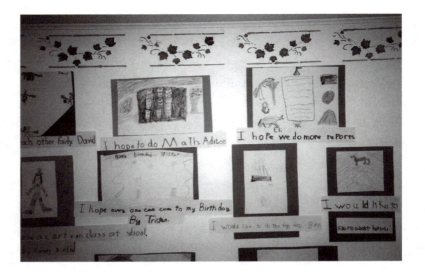

Teach
Children
How to
Choose Work

Teach Children How to Choose Work That is Worthy of Display

Children learn a lot through the process of choosing work for display. They learn to reflect on their work, to recognize effort and use it as a standard for judging whether work should be displayed, and to understand the value of growth in learning, not just the value of achieving perfection or mastering skills. The experience can also affirm their growing sense of competency and give them practice in individual and group decision making. Below is a process for teaching children how to choose work to display:

- *Discuss what helps children to learn.* Some examples of open-ended questions that can help children to deepen their understanding of their learning process are:

  When do you feel good about a piece of work you have done?
  When do you like to work hard on something?
  Do mistakes help you learn? How?
  Do other people help you learn? How?

- *Create criteria for choosing work to display.* Explore the question, "Why do we display work in our classroom?" Together, develop general guidelines for choosing work to display. These guidelines might include:

  The work shows our best efforts, not just perfect work.
  The work shows growth or improvement. (This may include displaying early drafts with later drafts.)
  We feel proud of the work.
  The work is important to us.

- *Practice choosing work for display.* Have students practice choosing a piece of work that fits the criteria for display. Ask children to share the thinking behind their choice. Classmates and the teacher can offer constructive feedback. Give children opportunities to practice using a number of different criteria. For example, have them choose a piece of work that shows growth, a piece that shows hard work, a piece that shows teamwork, etc.

- *Share work for display.* The first time students select a piece of their own work to display, ask them to share it with the class before putting it up. Students can point out aspects of the piece that they would like the class to notice. They can also invite questions or comments about their work.

- *Announce new displays.* Once children are regularly displaying their own work, they can make an announcement to the class whenever they have new work on display.

**Chapter
Five**

Teach Children How to Create Effective Displays

Effective displays celebrate each piece of work and radiate with a sense of student pride. They highlight the individual pieces of work rather than the surrounding decoration. Here are some ways to help children learn to create effective displays:

- *Remind students of the purposes of displaying work.* With a clear understanding of these purposes, children will be able to make clear, thoughtful decisions about what to display and how to display it.

- *Examine existing displays.* Take children to visit displays in the hallways and classrooms of the school. Consider visiting "real world" displays such as those in museums, storefronts, or libraries. Invite children to examine the effectiveness of these displays.
- *Create a list of qualities that make a display effective.* Using information the children have gathered from visiting various displays and the list of purposes of displays, create general guidelines for an effective display. For example:

1. Displays should be simple.
2. Displays should show what is most important in the work.
3. Decorations should fit with the piece of work and show it off.
4. Displays should include a label with the name of the student, a title, and perhaps something about the work.
5. Displays should be neat.

- *Post the guidelines near the art supplies used for making displays.* Include a supply of index cards and writing tools for creating labels.

After establishing these guidelines, students will be ready to learn some techniques to make displays beautiful and attention getting. You'll find these basic techniques on the following pages.

Techniques Children Can Use to Create Displays

Below are display techniques children can easily learn. As children become practiced in these techniques, they'll soon begin to improvise, creating their own styles. Make sure children always have easy access to the tools necessary for creating displays: a variety of art and writing materials, push pins, a stapler, and a staple remover.

Frames

Here are some simple ways for children to make frames:

- Use a stencil with a width of 1/4 inch, 1/2 inch, or 1 inch to draw a single or double line around the piece of work. After children become skilled at using a stencil, they can learn to use a ruler to create their own widths.

- Place the work on top of another piece of paper that is slightly larger and of a contrasting or complementary color, creating an outside frame. Provide many kinds of paper for this and encourage children to bring in further options (such as wallpaper samples, aluminum foil, and poster board).

- Cut out a frame, or a mat and frame, and attach the piece of work from behind, showing only the desired part of the work. This is a more advanced technique requiring the use of "frame and mat" stencils, either made by the teacher or donated from a local photography shop.

Once the work is framed, encourage students to consider the many possibilities for hanging it in the display area. They may want to hang pieces at different angles, in staggered steps, or in other interesting patterns.

Backdrops

Backdrops are a way of creating an accent and drawing the eye to a piece of work. Here are a few ways to make backdrops:

- Place pieces of paper or material of contrasting or complementary colors or shapes at angles behind the work.
- For three-dimensional pieces, students can try:
  - folding a piece of cardboard to create a standing screen
  - placing a cardboard box on its side to contain a scene
  - setting the piece on top of a cardboard box to create the feeling of displaying the piece on a stage or a pedestal
  - cutting windows in a box to create a viewing box

Techniques Children Can Use to Create Displays

Labels

Labels can be used to identify the theme of a display, to identify the creators of the work, or to capture the viewer's attention. Here are some simple techniques for making labels:

- Use a variety of shapes and colors of paper and a thin black marker.
- Use a computer to generate labels.
- Attach labels to displays in unusual ways. For example, tape a label to a straight pin and stick the pin into the displayed work at an angle to look like a flag.
- Use photographs to identify the creator of each work.
- Make labels look like comic book sentence bubbles.
- Craft the words on a label to entice the viewer to look at the display more closely. Including a question about the displayed work is often effective in drawing in the viewer.
- To make labels that can be placed next to three-dimensional displays, students can try:
  - making "tent cards" out of heavy-stock paper
  - writing information on an index card, inserting the card into a clothespin, pushing the two legs of the clothespin into a ball of modeling clay, then pressing the clay down on a horizontal surface
  - writing information on an index card and sliding the card into a small, rectangular holder (which you supply) with a slot cut down the middle lengthwise

Use Student Curators

Once children have learned how to choose work for displays and to display work effectively, they may be ready to take over the management of some of the display areas. By creating the role of a "student curator," a teacher can move the responsibility for overseeing many of the displays to the students.

The curator can be an individual, a pair of students, or even a small group of children. Curators might have the responsibility for a week, a month, or for the duration of a particular display.

Here are some possible student curator responsibilities:

- *Keep the area neat and beautiful.* The curator is responsible for making sure that nothing falls down, that corners are pinned flat, and that the display looks good in general.

- *Collect interactive work related to the display.* For example, a display might invite students to ask questions about the work displayed. Students would put their questions in an envelope in the display area, and the curator would collect the questions daily.

- *Oversee the creation of a display.* The curator makes sure that everyone responsible for a display does her/his job. In upper grade classrooms the curator might be in charge of creating a "blueprint" for the display area based on the number of children displaying and the kinds of work to be displayed. The curator might also decide how many pieces of work an area can hold.

- *Decide on a theme.* The curator chooses a particular theme for a display and manages the display area. Any student may then choose to participate in the theme display.

- *Organize a formal opening of the display.* Once a display is complete, the curator may hold an organized sharing time. During this sharing, the children displaying work would talk about their pieces and take questions and comments. The "audience" would be invited to visit the display during the day, then talk with the displayers about their work at the end of the day. The curator structures and manages this "grand opening."

Use Student Curators

Create Displays That Invite Interaction

Create Displays That Invite Interaction

In addition to celebrating students' accomplishments, displays should inspire questions and exploration. Here are a few ideas for displays that invite such interaction:

- *The question board or question box:* This is a place near the display where children can write questions they may have. For example, in a third grade class, small groups display what they have learned about specific animal habitats. Below each group's display is an empty area called the "question board." After studying the various displays, children write their questions on the question boards. These questions are later explored either in small groups or as a whole class. Using displays in this way creates excitement about the topics being studied.

- *Interactive exploration display:* Here, a set of materials or a piece of equipment is displayed on a table, where it can be examined and where discoveries can be recorded. For example, in a first grade classroom, the teacher conducts a guided exploration to introduce the class as a whole to a set of magnets. The children discover how the magnets might be used and cared for. The teacher then sets up a small table with enough space for three children at a time to explore the magnets further. On the table might be a container of magnets, a container of adjunct props, and paper and pencils. As children explore the magnets, they write down or illustrate their discoveries and post them on a small accompanying bulletin board.

- *Community brainstorming board:* This type of display consists of a poster, a chart, or a section of blackboard where a teacher or child poses a "Question of the Day" (or week). Children then have a period of time to respond to it in writing. This brainstorming board works best when it is a regular feature of the classroom and children know where, when, and how long it will be posted. At the end of the brainstorming period, the question and responses are brought to the group to share and discuss. I once visited a fifth grade class studying immigration to America. Each Tuesday the teacher wrote an open-ended, thought-provoking question about this topic on the Question-of-the-Week chart. The children could write their ideas on the chart until Friday morning, when the question was discussed as part of their social studies time. This display was successful partly because children had easy, daily access to the board and it was a routine activity in their classroom.

Chapter Five

FINE TUNINGS

Q. *Over the years I have accumulated some excellent posters that offer useful information about American history, a topic that fifth graders study in some depth. Are you suggesting that I should remove them from my walls because the children haven't made them?*

Fine Tunings

A. Absolutely not. Some manufactured posters can be very useful, especially when they are appropriate for the age, development, and interests of the children. I would certainly remove all the posters that have no meaningful connection to the curriculum. On the other hand, a store-made display showing all the U.S. presidents, for example, may be extremely useful and appropriate in a fifth grade classroom where children are studying American history. However, to keep interest high and avoid clutter, I would recommend that you keep the display up only during the time your class is studying presidents.

Q. *I feel frustrated with the lack of display space in my classroom. I have only two fixed bulletin boards: one large and one small, both by the door. I made an additional display board by attaching a thin sheet of steel, 2' x 3' and spray painted in a bright color, to the back of a freestanding bookshelf. The steel is magnetic, allowing children to hang their work with magnets and magnetic tape. Do you have any other suggestions for creating additional display space?*

A. Fortunately, there are many possibilities for creating display structures that are both easy to make and fairly inexpensive. In fact, the simple method you described can be used to turn the back of any bookshelf or free wall space into a bulletin board. Here are two additional ideas:

Create a freestanding bulletin board that can double as a room divider by simply taking a heavy sheet of pressed particleboard, Homasote, or corkboard and using four cinder blocks to stabilize it (two on each side of the board). Cover the board with flame retardant material or give it a few coats of bright paint, paint the blocks, and you'll have an attractive bulletin board that can be used in any part of the classroom.

Another idea is the "rain gutter" shelf. This shelf, made out of plastic rain gutter parts (one gutter section and two end pieces) and bolted to the wall, is particularly good for displaying students' published books, report folders, and class-made books. This idea came from Jim Trelease in his book, *The New Read-*

Aloud Handbook, and can be created relatively inexpensively. These shelves can be placed on any exposed wall and allow teachers to create displays at students' eye level.

Q. *The first and second graders I teach are very invested in creating their own displays. They put a lot of time and effort into choosing work for display and making the displays attractive. However, many of the written pieces and labels identifying work contain students' invented spelling mixed in with standard English spelling. How important is it that all labels and pieces of writing on display appear in standard English?*

A. Given that the emphasis of displays is on celebrating children's efforts and growth, rather than showcasing perfect work, I think it's fine for primary grade children to display work that includes invented spelling. Most important is that the work on display is meaningful to the children and meets the criteria of showing their best efforts.

That said, I do think it's a good idea to have a certain number of commonly used words, depending on the grade level, that students are expected to spell correctly in their work, including anything for display. There is also value in sometimes requiring children to do several drafts of a piece of writing in preparation for a display. Many teachers will do this, especially when preparing work for display outside of the classroom. However, to require that all writing on display be in perfect standard English could greatly limit the amount of work displayed and inhibit children's interest and excitement about displaying work.

Finally, on a related topic, I think it's important for students whose first language is not English to sometimes see their language of origin used in displays. Because students' identities are connected to their language and culture of origin, they will feel a greater sense of belonging if their language is reflected in the classroom. For example, a display in a first grade classroom on families might include labels that identify members of families in various languages. Or in a fourth grade classroom where children are keeping a list of all the games they are learning, the games could be listed in English as well as other languages.

Chapter Six

Ambience is not easy to define or describe, yet most people know within minutes of entering a place whether the ambience is right for them. Does the place make them feel comfortable or tense? Stimulated or bored? Welcome or alienated? Ambience is the feeling or mood associated with a particular place. It involves our emotional response to a place and how that place affects all our senses.

A classroom's ambience makes a difference in how well children learn. While it's impossible to create an environment that is pleasing to everyone *all* of the time—each child's response will be unique—it is possible to create one that is pleasing to most children *most* of the time. The goal is to make the environment welcoming, comfortable, and engaging.

The details of how to do this vary greatly depending on the teacher's style and the makeup of the school community. I recently visited a third grade classroom in Pennsylvania in which the teacher, along with students, had transformed the entire classroom into an imaginary ship sailing around the world. Drawing upon a lifelong passion for travel, the teacher had taught students how to read maps and make beautiful maps of their own, many of which were displayed on the classroom walls. A small wooden lighthouse with room for two or three children inside served as a quiet reading area. The daily written message to students often began with the salutation, "Ahoy, Sailors!" And each week, a new student took on the responsibilities of the captain of the ship, including taking attendance, checking cleanup, and leading Morning Meeting. It was a playful and inviting classroom—warm, engaging, and fun—and it worked well for this particular group of children.

While a teacher's passions should never dominate a classroom, they certainly are critical to enlivening its ambience and sparking students' excitement about learning. Some of the most engaging classrooms I've been in are the ones in which the teacher's passions—whether for art, history, poetry, or the natural world—are obvious and reflected in the physical setup of the room.

Almost every decision a teacher makes regarding the arrangement of the classroom will have some impact on its ambience. The way a teacher arranges the desks or tables, the height and location of shelves, the design of entryways, the arrangement of displays, the placement of the teacher's desk, and how materials are stored will all contribute to the overall feeling of the room.

Goals of Creating Ambience

Classroom ambience is also greatly influenced by the sensory experience the environment offers: the sounds and smells, the light and colors, the visual and tactile textures, the temperature, and the ventilation of the place. Finally, the intellectual atmosphere of the classroom will influence its ambience. Is this a classroom where children feel comfortable taking risks? Are they and their teacher excited about what they're learning? Is learning fun and infectious?

Goals of Creating Ambience

The ambience of a classroom changes naturally over the course of the school year as seasons come and go, old displays come down and new ones go up, and the class moves on to new materials and topics of study. But through it all, the goals to keep in mind as you consider ambience should stay the same—to create a classroom that is:

- **Welcoming—The classroom makes children feel welcome as individuals and as a community of learners.**

- **Comfortable—The classroom provides children with a sense of comfort and security.**

- **Engaging—The classroom is interesting and stimulating while not being overwhelming.**

GETTING STARTED

Much of what's been addressed in previous chapters regarding the selection and arrangement of furniture, materials, and displays applies here as well. A classroom where children feel a strong sense of belonging, ownership, and engagement as individuals and as a community of learners, where furniture is appropriately sized and materials are accessible, where displays reflect children's identities, interests and accomplishments, will be a classroom with a pleasant ambience.

What follows are suggestions for improving ambience which have not been covered in other chapters, with the bulk of the suggestions focusing on factors affecting the five senses—sight, hearing, smell, touch, and taste.

Make the Entrance Inviting

Chapter Six

First impressions count. The entrance to a classroom should be warm and welcoming. It should be free of clutter and obstructions and should beckon visitors inside. Here are some suggestions for creating an inviting entrance:

- *Display photographs of the class or of each child individually on the door or just inside the door.* Include individual children's names and words of welcome.

- *Display a poster of "welcoming words" on the door, such as "Greetings! Welcome to second grade. Please come in!"* For the opening days of school, you can provide the words yourself. Then, during the first week of school, you might invite the children to create their own welcome sign to replace yours. In classrooms where there are students learning English as a second language, it is important to include "welcoming words" in their languages of origin.

- *Assign one child each week to be the official greeter.* Post this child's name and photo on the welcome sign. For example, the sign might read, "Welcome, visitors! Knock once and then come right in. Jamie, our official greeter, will help you."

Consider How the Environment Affects the Five Senses

Sense of Sight

Light

Light can influence children's emotional well-being and their ability to read comfortably. To improve the lighting, teachers can:

- *Make sure that the lights are working properly.* Flickering fluorescent lights are distracting, hurt eyesight, cause headaches, and can lead to problem behaviors.

- *If possible, request that full-spectrum fluorescent bulbs be used in fluorescent fixtures.* Since this type of lighting more closely resembles natural light, it is better for the eyes and can improve concentration.

- *Add table lamps or floor lamps in areas where small groups or individual children work.* This creates a sense of warmth and coziness.

- *Be aware of how the sun streams into the room during different times of the day and year.* While the sun can bring in wonderful light, bright sunlight can be distracting. If the sun shines directly onto work surfaces, into children's eyes, or onto a blackboard to create a blinding reflection, then the classroom should have window shades.

- *Make sure the windows are clean, inside and out.* Dirty windows can block a surprising amount of light. Cleaning the windows can be a fun way for children to help in the maintenance of the classroom.

Color

Color affects the way people respond to an environment. Colors may be warm or cool, calming or stimulating. The all-too-familiar institutional greens, beiges, and yellows of our classrooms rarely create a feeling of warmth or excitement. While you may not be able to paint your room or choose the color, you can use splashes of color to improve the ambience.

Chapter Six

- *Use bright shades of red, blue, yellow, or green to paint bulletin boards, free-standing bookcases, tables, and even the trim of the blackboards.* Be careful not to paint too much trim, especially around windows and in small classrooms. This can create a choppy look. In a very small classroom it is better to keep most of the walls and window trims all the same color (preferably white or off-white) to give the illusion of a bigger space.

- *Use brightly colored material to make window curtains, to cover a bulletin board, or to cover pillows.* But remember that the purpose of the color is to create an accent, not to become the focus itself. Choose a brightly colored material that doesn't have an overly busy pattern. Many commercial materials made for children are too distracting for the classroom.

- *Choose a low-pile area rug in a bright color to create an active work area or an inviting whole-class meeting area.* Again, remember that the color and design should not become the focus.

- *For carpeting, pillows, and bookcases in a quiet area, use pale or pastel colors such as light green, peach, or light blue.*

- *Use soft pastel colors for an area where children resolve conflicts and solve problems.*

- *Use colored frames and mats to display and draw interest to children's work.*

Plants

Plants set on a windowsill or hung from a wall can help give a classroom a "homey" feeling. Taller floor plants, used as a natural screen, can create a private corner to which children can retreat when they need a quiet place.

In addition, plants can improve the air quality by using the carbon dioxide that we exhale and giving us clean oxygen in return. However, if they are not dusted and watered regularly, plants can have the opposite health effect, spreading dust mites and molds. Worse still, a classroom filled with dried-up, leafless, or dying plants can give children the wrong message—that this is a place where living things are neglected. It's far better to have one or two plants that are well cared for than to have lots of plants that are neglected.

Sense of Sound

Noise level

Consider How the Environment Affects the Five Senses

In an active classroom where children are learning through hands-on activities and interactions with their peers, there will always be a certain amount of productive noise. When this healthy hum gets too loud, however, children can have difficulty focusing and learning. As a general rule, the noise level is productive if no one has to shout or talk over the noise in order to be heard, regardless of where s/he is in the room. Children can be taught to be sensitive to the noise level in the classroom and to adjust their volumes when necessary. But there are also some design strategies that will help keep the noise level productive:

- *Locate work areas near others with a similar noise level.*

- *Create quiet spaces with a few headphones or earmuffs and a desk or two that can be set apart from other desks and activities.* Children can use these areas when they are feeling distracted. This is particularly useful for children with attention difficulties.

- *Make sure that all movable furniture moves quietly.* This is especially important in classrooms with tile or linoleum floors and chairs with metal feet. One way to cut the scraping sound from chairs being pushed in and out is to put old tennis balls or small felt pads on the feet of the chairs. If desks need to be moved daily to set up a whole-class meeting area, then the feet of the desk legs should be covered as well.

Music

A classroom filled with music can be comforting and engaging to children while also teaching them about sound, rhythm, harmony, and mood. Research shows that music enhances children's intellectual development and prepares them for learning. (Weinberger 1998, 39) Here are some ideas for bringing music into the classroom:

- *Provide a collection of musical instruments children can use to create their own music.* Include different kinds of rhythm and tone instruments (bells, chimes, and tone bars), each with its own storage area and plastic bag or container. Keeping them jumbled together in a basket often suggests that it is acceptable just to throw the instruments into the basket. Establish a music corner where instruments can be used without disturbing others.

- *Invest in a good tape or CD player to be used for whole-class activities.* The quality of the sound is important to using this tool effectively. Put the equipment where you can easily access it.

- *Create a listening station on a table, a desk, or the floor, with at least one tape or CD player and two sets of earphones.* In upper grades, you may want to allow children to take a player and a set of earphones to a place of their choice and return the equipment when they're finished.

- *Have a broad range of music—classical, jazz, blues, rock, folk—to share with children.* Encourage children to bring in music that reflects their culture and family background. Play this music for the whole class as well as making it available for the classroom listening station.

- *Encourage children to create and record their own songs and music by supplying the music area with lined music paper, pencils, and blank tapes.* You can also keep some blank paper and drawing tools in the music area so children can draw as they listen.

- *Use a drum to create rhythms for moving around the room during transitions or to lead brief stretching breaks throughout the day.* Also, use a drum, bell, or chime to signal the children that it is time to freeze where they are, stop what they're doing, and give you or another student their attention.

The intercom

When the intercom is used excessively, as it is in many schools, it becomes a distracting noise that interrupts learning. Although the individual classroom teacher usually has no direct control over the use of the intercom, teachers can advocate for reducing its use. Encourage the use of daily or weekly administration memos. News and information that applies to the children can be part of a written morning message that greets children as they enter the building. Alternatively, the teacher or a class messenger can pick up news from the office every day and share it with the class.

Sense of Smell

Children will concentrate best in an environment that is clean and odor-free. In addition to avoiding cleaners and art materials that give off strong smells, pay attention to any strong odor in the classroom and investigate its source. A musty smell might mean that the ventilation system is not working properly. In old school buildings, it might also mean that too much dust has collected and it's time to vacuum the walls, ceilings, and bookshelves, in addition to the floors.

Be aware, too, of children's particular sensitivities. Something as simple as a teacher's perfume might affect a child's ability to concentrate or even cause allergic reactions. Chapter Seven will provide more in-depth information about ways to improve air quality in the classroom.

Sense of Touch

Temperature

Hot classrooms can make students sleepy, irritable, or cranky. Cold classrooms can make it difficult for children to write, draw, or sit still. Low humidity can aggravate asthma, sinus problems, and ear infections. Eric Jensen, author of *Teaching with the Brain in Mind,* states that "the brain's optimal physical environment includes a temperature near 70 degrees and a humidity level near 70 percent." (Jensen 1998, 42)

While many factors affecting the temperature and humidity in a classroom are beyond an individual teacher's control, teachers can become advocates for addressing temperature issues school-wide. One example of teachers doing this successfully comes from a school in Cincinnati, Ohio. The school had no air conditioning, and during the early and late months of the school year, temperatures became beastly in the classrooms. Teachers would open the windows to let in cooler air, but because the school was surrounded by grassy fields, this also brought in dozens of bees. A few years ago, a group of teachers, advocating for the safety and health of the children, were able to get the superintendent and school board to budget resources to add screens to the windows.

In addition to speaking out for improved physical conditions school-wide, there are simple steps that teachers can take to improve the climate in the classroom:

Chapter Six

- *Be informed about the heating and cooling system in your school.*

  With an understanding of the system, you can make sure that the design and layout of your classroom is not causing an uncomfortable climate. Simple problems such as furniture blocking a heat source or materials covering an air blower are easy to fix.

- *Address problems proactively whenever possible.*

  If the room is hot:

  - Open windows (if possible), but not those directly over the heating system or thermostat.

  - Place small, quiet, oscillating fans in one or two strategic places low to the ground to blow the cooler air around.

  - If windows open, use window fans to draw in cool air. Be sure to choose quiet fans to avoid a noise problem.

  - Use window shades to help block the heat of the sun.

  - If you open windows, use screens whenever possible to keep out bees and wasps.

  If the room is cold or drafty:

  - Inform families so that children come to school dressed in layers. Being aware of the issue, families can also become advocates for addressing the problem with administrators.

  - Locate children's work areas away from drafty areas.

If the temperature is uneven, with hot and cold spots:

- Place small, quiet, oscillating fans in one or two strategic places to circulate the air.

If the room is dry:

- Place an electrostatic humidifier in one or two central spots in the classroom. These humidifiers have improved technology that allows them to produce a warm mist free of allergens and impurities. It's important to wash the humidifier thoroughly at least once a week with water and vinegar.

Textures

Consider How the Environment Affects the Five Senses

Having a variety of textures in a classroom can make the environment more interesting and stimulating for children. There are some health risks associated with carpeting and other textured surfaces (see Chapter Seven), so it's important to proceed cautiously in this area. Learn about possible health hazards before deciding on an option. Here are a few suggestions for providing a variety of textures in the classroom:

- *Furniture*
  - Provide textured seating with covers that can either be wiped clean or removed and washed. Examples are bean bag chairs, wicker chairs, nylon floor seats, polyester cushioned floor seats, hanging rope hammock chairs, wooden benches with or without foam pads, large foam pillows, and foam mattresses.
  - Provide work surfaces with a variety of textures. A rectangular piece of marble or granite the size of a cutting board, a finely sanded and oiled wood surface, and a melamine-coated Masonite sheet are all interesting writing surfaces.
  - Use a small washable cotton throw rug to add a little texture and comfort to a reading or writing nook.

- *Learning materials*
  - Provide materials that offer a wide range of textures, such as fabric, yarn, string, straws, feathers, wood pieces, buttons, ribbons, cotton, and cardboard. Also include materials that can be mixed to create textured work, such as papier-mâché and finger paint. If you use balls

for Morning Meeting greetings and activities, choose balls with a variety of textures, such as Koosh Balls, gel-filled balls, tennis balls, blow-up beach balls, and foam balls.

- In primary classrooms, provide materials of different textures—such as sand, beans, water, cornstarch, and a cornstarch and water mixture—for measuring and exploring volume.

- In older children's classrooms, offer a variety of math manipulatives, textured globes and maps, items from nature (rocks, driftwood, nests, etc.), or other materials that invite students to explore through touch.

- *Decorations*
  - Encourage children to display artwork with different textures that others can touch.

  - As a class, make classroom decorations or displays that involve different textures (for example, a class quilt, a woven multi-textured wall hanging, or a multi-textured mobile).

  - Use curtains, tablecloths, or even equipment covers to add variety to the textures in the room.

- *Animals*
  - Different animals can provide a broad range of textures from scaly smooth to feathery soft. However, it is critical to know the allergies of the children in the classroom before making decisions about animals. See Chapter Seven for an in-depth discussion of whether to have animals in the classroom.

Chapter Six

Sense of Taste

Water

For physical comfort and well-being, children need drinking water throughout the day. If the classroom has a sink with running water, you can provide small disposable paper cups or ask children to each bring in a cup. Children can hang their cups on individual hooks on the wall.

If your classroom doesn't have running water, you can create a system for keeping track of when children leave the room to get a drink. Some teachers leave a box filled with name cards next to the door and place above it two signs ("Restroom" and "Fountain"), with one or two hooks under each. When leaving the room, a child places her/his name card under the appropriate sign. Alternatively, teachers can keep bottled water and cups in the room or keep an individual water bottle for each child.

Food

To keep energy and attention levels high, children need food throughout the day. Recent brain research has shown that it's critical for children of all ages to have regular snacks during the school day for optimum learning. (Jensen 1998, 42) Many early childhood and some primary grade classrooms have regular snack times; it's equally important to provide snack opportunities for older students throughout the day.

Consider How the Environment Affects the Five Senses

One way to provide occasional snacks while also creating a "homey" feeling in the classroom is to cook with children regularly. Cooking can make a classroom smell wonderful, enrich the curriculum, and build a sense of community. If you cook on a regular basis, you'll need a supply of simple cooking tools, such as mixing bowls, wooden spoons, measuring spoons and cups, a couple of small cutting boards, and appropriate knives. Multiple tools are important so more than one child can work at a task. You may also want to keep a supply of paper plates and napkins. Store cooking tools together, in a cabinet or in a closed plastic bin on a shelf. If the room has a sink, store the cooking materials near it. The school kitchen may also provide cooking tools or storage space.

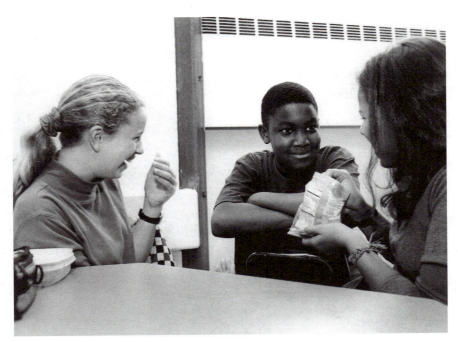

Whether you plan to cook regularly with children or simply provide a space and time for daily snacks, here are some design implications to keep in mind:

- If you plan to keep a supply of foods (pretzels, popcorn, crackers, peanut butter, etc.) for occasional snacks, store them in tightly closed containers out of sight so they stay fresh and bug-free and do not become a temptation.

- If children take turns providing a snack for the class, you will need a permanent storage area away from the main activity and traffic flow of the classroom.

- If children decide for themselves when they want to eat a snack, the following arrangements allow them to eat while others continue to work:

  - *Designate a snack table.* Use a small table or desk that can seat at least three or four children. When a seat is available, a child gets his/her snack and comes to the snack table to eat.

  - *Have children eat at their own workspace.* When a child is ready to have a snack, the child clears off her/his workspace. If all the desks or tables are used as community workspaces, then children may choose any empty workspace for eating.

  - *Let older children choose where to eat.* Older children can often handle eating in any part of the classroom after the class has discussed appropriate places for various foods.

- If everyone is moving at the same time to get snacks and clean up, it's likely that there will be traffic jams. You can minimize this by either releasing children in a staggered fashion or by keeping snacks and cleanup supplies in different parts of the room. Make sure you provide enough sponges, paper towels, dustpans, and brooms so children can clean up from snack quickly and efficiently.

Chapter Six

FINE TUNINGS

Q. *Bright sunlight comes into our classroom everyday, shining into children's eyes. I can't get curtains right away due to tight budgets. What can I do in the meantime?*

A. Until you are able to get curtains, one thing you can do is tape translucent paper, such as large sheets of newsprint, to the windows where the sun comes in. This will let light in but will diffuse it. When you do get curtains, be sure to get ones that you can open and close easily. Finally, since the sun comes in a window at different angles at different times of the year, sometimes it is simplest to make a slight adjustment in the design of the classroom. Moving a group of desks or not using a particular area at certain times may be a fine temporary solution.

Fine Tunings

Q. *I would like to have either a stage or a loft in our classroom. What are the advantages and disadvantages of each?*

A. Many teachers like having stages, platforms, or lofts in the classroom. These offer variety in workspaces and give children the opportunity to experience their classroom from different angles and heights. Seeing the world from different physical perspectives can build children's capacity to think from different perspectives as well. However, lofts and stages require the skills of an experienced carpenter, and many schools restrict or even prohibit their use due to fire regulations and/or accessibility concerns.

A stage or platform is much lower to the ground than a loft and easier to build. While it still offers children a change in perspective, it can be used by a child with limited mobility because it is low to the ground and doesn't have railings. When the stage or platform is small (2' x 2' to 3' x 3'), a classroom might have as many as three of them, all at different heights and grouped together to create a multi-level environment.

A loft is more complicated to build, but it creates a significant amount of additional space in the classroom. It's possible for a carpenter to build a loft using bolts so you can easily take the loft apart and remove it if you move to another classroom or if you need to make the classroom accessible to a child who uses a wheelchair.

Many children love the exhilarating feeling that comes from being up high, looking out over the rest of the world. They also enjoy snuggling in to read, write, or play a quiet game with a friend. If you decide to build a loft, make sure you use open lattice walls so you can see into the loft from several places in the classroom.

You can also create a small room underneath a loft. In addition to the doorway, try to give the room windows, so children can enjoy the cozy feeling that comes from being inside a space while at the same time being able to look out from within it. Besides providing another opportunity for perspective taking, the windows and doorway allow the teacher to see inside.

Q. *I like your ideas about bringing music into the classroom and would like to allow children to play instruments, but I think it might be too disturbing to others. What are your thoughts on this?*

A. Bob Strachota, a teacher at the Greenfield Center School, came up with a wonderful solution to just this problem. Using his carpentry skills, he built a small, soundproof cubicle big enough for two or three children in a corner of the classroom. He had two purposes: He wanted the children to be able to create music as part of their curriculum throughout the day, and he wanted to give children a place to practice their recorders since he was teaching the whole class how to play. It took a lot of work to build the cubicle, but the space worked beautifully.

Chapter Six

Q. *I'm thinking about bringing one of my old sofas into the classroom in order to create a warmer ambience. What are your thoughts on this?*

A. Teachers, the most enthusiastic recyclers of all, often like to bring a big, old comfy chair or sofa into the classroom rather than throw it away. While a sofa or chair can provide a sense of comfort, I suggest you approach this decision with caution by asking yourself the following:

- Is there ample space in the classroom for this piece of furniture without compromising any of the other learning spaces?

- Have you considered the possible health risks? If you have any upholstered furniture in the classroom, it is extremely important that the upholstery be thoroughly and regularly cleaned. Many teachers partially address this issue by covering the furniture with an easily washable slipcover.

- Is the size of this sofa right for the classroom and the students? If the children are young (four to seven years old), chances are the sofa will overwhelm the rest of the furniture, even if there is space for it. Consider instead purchasing a few bean bag chairs that two children can sit in comfortably, or some child-sized furniture.

Chapter Seven

MAKING IT HEALTHY, KEEPING IT CLEAN

In the last twenty years educators have become increasingly aware of the silent dangers that lurk inside the ventilation systems, custodial closets, supply closets, and carpets of our classrooms and schools. Toxic cleaning supplies, fumes from art materials, mold, mildew, and dust can all seriously compromise children's and teachers' health and well-being, making it difficult to concentrate on teaching and learning.

Children are especially vulnerable to environmental health hazards. Because they are still growing and have faster metabolisms than adults, their bodies absorb toxins more readily. Per pound of body weight, children also eat, drink, and breathe more than adults. Finally, their behavior, such as frequently putting their hands and materials into their mouths, exposes them to more environmental threats than adults. (Healthy Schools Network 1999, 2)

Therefore, choosing healthy materials and keeping the classroom as clean and pollutant free as possible are of critical importance. The issues involved, however, are admittedly complex and may seem overwhelming for one teacher to address. For example, there are many factors affecting the indoor air quality in the classroom, such as temperature, humidity, and maintenance of air ducts, which teachers have little control over. Also, the best solutions to these problems often require money that communities cannot, or will not, spend.

Nevertheless, there are many things that individual teachers can do to improve the air quality and overall healthiness of the classroom environment. The goal is not to create the "perfect" environment or an environment that's so sterile that it's devoid of any interesting materials, but to create a classroom that is as safe and healthy as possible while still being welcoming, interesting, and conducive to learning.

I recommend that teachers stay informed of current health issues, learn about the needs of the specific group of children they're teaching, and take appropriate action as needed. This chapter offers suggestions, guidelines, and resources for making a classroom as clean, nontoxic, pollutant free, and allergen free as possible.

GETTING STARTED

Common Health Hazards in the Classroom: Problems and Solutions

There is a wealth of information on classroom health hazards, with new findings constantly being released. While addressing all the areas of environmental health concerns is beyond the scope of this book, I can offer facts about some of the most common health hazards in the classroom and suggest ways to remedy them. At the end of this chapter is a list of resources if you'd like to educate yourself further. In addition, Appendix C offers an extensive list of art materials and projects that are safe for children and other high-risk individuals.

Temperature, Humidity, and Ventilation

The problem: The biggest problem related to temperature, humidity, and ventilation is that they're all too often beyond the teacher's control. As a result, classrooms are often too hot, too cold, too dry, or too stuffy for students' and teachers' comfort. In addition to making children and adults uncomfortable, these conditions can aggravate asthma, sinus problems, colds, and infections.

What you can do: Although truly addressing temperature, humidity, and ventilation problems may require a school-wide change, there are things that individual teachers can do to make improvements to the climate in the classroom. I offer specific ideas in Chapter Six.

Cleaning Products

The problem: Many cleaning products commonly used in the classroom contain industrial strength chemicals that are hazardous to breathe and touch.

Many also contain disinfectants made with toxic pesticides that are not necessary for basic, everyday cleaning.

What you can do:

- Avoid products that contain harmful chemicals and disinfectants. A simple solution of vinegar and water works well for most everyday cleaning, such as wiping tables or desks. If children do use chemical cleaners, insist that they wear rubber gloves.

- Advocate for the use of healthier cleaning supplies school-wide. There are two excellent resources on this topic: Healthy Schools Network publishes a pamphlet titled "Healthier Cleaning and Maintenance Practices and Products for Schools" (for a copy, call 1-518-462-0632 or visit www.hsnet.org); and Janitorial Products Pollution Prevention Project provides fact sheets on the relative safety and hazards of industrial cleaning products of all kinds (for information, visit www.westp2net.org/Janitorial/jp4.htm).

Chapter Seven

Sponges

The problem: Sponges harbor germs, cultivate them rapidly, and then spread them from surface to surface.

What you can do:

- Wash sponges every day.
- Provide different sponges for use on the floor, tables, and dishes. Create a system that clearly identifies which sponges should be used for what. For example, green sponges might be used for the floors, blue sponges for tables, and pink sponges for dishes. Each color sponge would have its own labeled tray identifying its particular use.
- Put out fresh sponges regularly.
- Use Handiwipes instead.

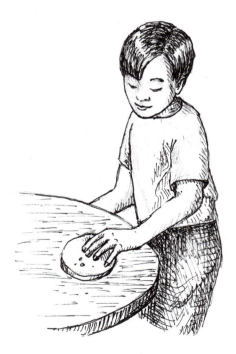

Markers

The problem: Permanent felt-tip markers, dry-erase markers, and other solvent-containing markers (these often have strong smells) contain volatile organics that are dangerous for children to breathe.

What you can do:

- Use markers that are water-based and labeled nontoxic.
- For dry-erase markers, an option is a product by Crayola called Color Wipeoffs. They are nontoxic, washable, and odor free (many nontoxic dry-erase markers still have a strong odor).

Problems and Solutions

Glue

The problem: Certain types of glue, such as rubber cement, contain a toxic chemical called naphtha. Rubber cement containing naphtha, used widely for many years for gluing paper, is now banned from elementary classrooms. In recent years, several good nontoxic substitutes have come on the market. They provide the same quality and strength without the toxic exposure.

What you can do:

- For general paper gluing, I prefer glue sticks because a thin coat of these glues is all it takes to hold things firmly. Some glue sticks allow both permanent and removable gluing. Others allow you to rub off excess glue while it's drying without damaging the paper.
- You can use double-sided tape, nontoxic rubber cement, or any other solvent-free glue.

Carpeting

The problem: Wall-to-wall carpeting can produce several serious environmental health problems. First, the synthetics used to make the carpeting and its padding, the floor preparation compounds and sealers, and the adhesive used to attach the carpet to the floor can all cause air quality problems. Second, mold and mildew develop in old carpeting as a result of roof leaks, high humidity, and wet shoes. Third, carpets collect pesticides and metal dust from shoes, and these can stay in the carpet for long periods of time. Fourth, carpeting provides a haven for pollen, dust mites, and lice. (MassCOSH 1996)

What you can do:

- Remove wall-to-wall carpeting whenever possible. Do not install it in a new or renovated building. Instead, use one or two low-pile area carpets or rug squares that can be cleaned and/or replaced regularly. Place area rugs away from heavy traffic areas, such as pathways near doors.

  If new carpeting is installed,

- Follow safety recommendations for airing out new carpeting.

- Clean carpets daily by vacuuming with cleaners equipped with high efficiency particulate air (HEPA) filters; clean spills as soon as they occur; and shampoo regularly with a nontoxic carpet shampoo.

- Use preventive strategies to keep dirt, water, and dust out of the carpet. Here are a few possibilities:

  1. Ask children to bring a pair of shoes or slippers to use inside the classroom only. Children change out of these shoes whenever they go outside (except during an emergency or a fire drill).

  2. Have children leave boots or outdoor shoes in the hallway. Children can make paper outlines of their boots or shoes, decorate them and label them with their name. Laminate these and tape them along the wall in the hallway so each child has a set spot for his/her shoes. If children have lockers in the hallway, they can keep their indoor and outdoor shoes in the lockers.

  3. Have children sit in chairs or on washable seating mats (these can be made inexpensively out of oil cloth or plastic tarp) to reduce skin contact with the carpeting. Wipe the mats at least once a week.

Upholstered Furniture

The problem: Upholstered furniture, including throw pillows, whether new or used, present some of the same health concerns as carpeting. Upholstery tends to be a haven for dust mites and lice and is even more difficult to clean than carpeting. In addition, some upholstery is made of synthetic materials that can pollute the air.

What you can do:

- Remove upholstered furniture. Many environmental safety organizations recommend banning all upholstered furniture from the classroom. Given the safety risks and the fact that upholstered furniture often takes up an inordinate amount of space, getting rid of it may be the best choice for the classroom.

- Replace an upholstered "comfy" chair with a comfortable non-upholstered chair. Wooden or wicker rockers, Adirondack chairs, plastic inflatable chairs, and bean bag chairs with removable, washable covers are all available in child-sized versions. There are other comfortable chairs that don't take up a lot of space and can be easily folded up and stored. These include camping chairs, "butterfly" chairs which have a washable canvas seat over a metal frame, and "director's" chairs which have a removable canvas seat and back. Many of these are available in all-purpose stores, camping stores, and stores selling children's and outdoor furniture.

- If you don't have any students who are highly allergic and you don't have a serious, continuous battle with lice, it may be fine to have a comfortable upholstered chair in the classroom if it's covered with a washable cotton slipcover. The cover needs to be washed frequently, and this may be more work than it's worth. Also, the slipcover will not protect children from any toxins in synthetic upholstery material.

- Use throw pillows or large foam pillows or pads to sit on in place of upholstered furniture. Pillows and foam pads are easier to clean and take up less space than an upholstered chair. Choose nonallergenic foam pillows and pads; cover them with removable, washable cotton covers; and wash the covers frequently.

Animals

The problem: Feathered and furry animals, such as birds and hamsters, give children practice in caring for a living creature, offer opportunities to study animal habits and behavior, and give children a chance to experience love, attachment, and empathy. However, feathered and furry animals can also cause health problems. Besides having dander that causes allergic reactions in some children, these animals create sanitation problems and attract insects.

What you can do:

- Do not have feathered or furry animals in the classroom, especially if any children are allergic to these animals. Many environmental safety organizations recommend banning all feathered and furry animals from classrooms.

- Choose a snake, turtle, or frog for a class pet, or get a fish tank.

- If you don't have any children who are allergic to animal dander, it is possible to have a bird or furry animal in the classroom without creating health problems if you are vigilant about animal care, handling, and cleaning. The best place to clean animal cages is in the custodian's utility sink. However, you can use a classroom sink if there's no water fountain in it and if the sink is cleaned properly afterwards with a safe cleaning product. Here are a few additional guidelines to follow:

  1. Cages should be cleaned at least once a week.

  2. If children are helping with the cleaning, they should wear rubber gloves and a filter mask to protect them from contact with animal wastes.

  3. Dispose of soiled sawdust, wood chips, or newspaper in a tightly closed plastic garbage bag. Immediately take the bag from the classroom to the school dumpster. Always wash cages before putting in fresh sawdust, wood chips, or newspaper.

  4. Keep an oilcloth folded next to the animal cage for children to put on their laps or on the floor when they hold or play with the animals. This protects the children, furniture, and floor from animal waste. If the oilcloth gets soiled, wipe it clean with a damp paper towel immediately.

  5. Children should wash their hands immediately after handling any animal.

Computer Video Display Terminals (VDTs)

The problem: There has been a tremendous amount of concern in recent years over the health and safety hazards associated with the use of VDTs. Some of these concerns include eye problems, muscle strain, and low- and high-frequency radiation fields emitted by VDTs.

Eye Problems

- Eyestrain, blurred vision, and nearsightedness are a few of the eye problems that can result from VDT use. Problems arise from improper lighting, excessive glare, and prolonged staring at the screen. (VDT Health and Safety Fact Sheet 1993) Children's eyes are in particular danger during the primary years when their eye muscles are still developing. Too much early eyestrain can lead to nearsightedness before children leave the third grade. (Gesell, Ilg, and Bullis 1998)

Muscle Strain

- VDT use may cause muscle strain in the neck, back, shoulders, arms, hands, and wrists. The problems arise from repetitive motion on the keyboard, improper posture, and improper placement of the computer station. While most of these problems occur in adults who spend long hours at the computer, it's worth paying attention to these problems in children as well.

Problems and Solutions

Radiation

- In 1993 tests conducted by OSHA (The Occupational Safety and Health Administration) showed that radiation levels from VDT use were well below those allowed by current standards. (U.S. Department of Labor 1993, 1) However, the OSHA standards were established for adults and the tests were conducted on adults. We already know from other health and safety standards that children are far more susceptible to environmental hazards than adults. Since there is still much that we don't know about the radiation effects of VDTs on children, it seems wise to take some precautions as to where, how, and how much we use VDTs in the classroom.

What you can do:

- Minimize the number of computers in the classroom and use them sparingly and wisely. The computer is a vital tool for learning, but it is only one of many tools.

- Turn computers off when they're not in use. In most classrooms I visit, computers are turned on first thing in the morning and turned off only when the teacher leaves at the end of the day. The dangers of low-level radiation are reduced if computers are turned off when they're not in use.

- Purchase only VDT equipment with shielding to reduce radiation emissions.

- To minimize exposure to radiation, place VDTs so that the back of the terminal is against a wall, the back of a bookcase, or a solid divider.

- Minimize muscle strain by teaching children to use proper posture and to sit at an adequate distance from the screen. Make sure the screen is at the children's eye level. The best way to do this is to use tables with separate adjustable platforms for the screen and the keyboard.

- Provide good lighting to minimize eyestrain.

- To minimize glare, place computer terminals at right angles to windows, cover windows, or provide antiglare screens.

Be Aware of Students' Sensitivities and Allergies

Knowing students' specific allergies or sensitivities will help you make informed and healthy design choices in the classroom. A good place to start is to check students' files. You may also want to send a letter home in the summer asking for information about any allergies or sensitivities, and in some cases, meet with families to learn more about children's symptoms, allergy "triggers," and preventive measures.

You should also learn to recognize the general symptoms of allergies and sensitivities, so that a child who has not been diagnosed can get the care and attention s/he needs. Remember that, among many other things, children can be sensitive to noise, light, activity, odors, touch, and food. Three approaches can help you detect allergies and sensitivities:

1. Be ready to ask the questions that might point to an allergy or sensitivity.

When a child is behaving in ways that seem uncharacteristic or that are getting in the way of his/her learning, always be prepared to ask whether there might be a physical allergy or sensitivity at play.

2. Listen to children and observe behavior patterns.

Children provide us with a constant source of information about the classroom environment. For example, a child might complain consistently about a particular smell, revealing an environmental sensitivity. Or s/he might exhibit nervous energy every day after lunch, a possible sign of a food allergy.

When observing and interpreting children's physical symptoms, however, it can be difficult to decipher what is real, what is imagined, and what is real but exaggerated in its seriousness. Take the seven-year-old, for example, who complains daily about a headache or stomachache. While this should be taken seriously, it's also important to understand that children this age have a developmental tendency to feel anxieties about themselves, and that these anxieties often result in physical symptoms such as headaches or stomachaches. In this case, the teacher should gather as much information as possible by documenting when the headaches or stomachaches occur, how long they last, and what connections, if any, they have to other events in the classroom. While it's important to interpret this information within the context of the child's development, it's also important never to overlook or dismiss these signals.

3. Listen to the child's family.

Be Aware of Students' Sensitivities and Allergies

In some cases, children share their complaints with their family instead of their teacher, or it's the family that notices an unhealthy behavior pattern. It is important to work with the family, acknowledging their concern and taking steps to investigate the issue. Be careful that you don't take the family's concern as a personal attack on what you have chosen to put or use in the classroom. The setup of the classroom should be an evolving process, with revisions and fine tunings made throughout the year as you learn more about the needs of each student.

Keeping the Classroom Clean

A major challenge in active, hands-on classrooms is to allow for learning that requires lots of "messing about" while also keeping the environment clean. The classroom does not have to be sterile, but the more dust free and germ free the better. While most schools have custodians who help keep the classrooms clean, there are steps teachers can take in setting up the room that will make cleanups easier.

Keep the amount of furniture and materials to an appropriate minimum.

As noted in earlier chapters, having excessive furniture and materials makes it difficult to keep floors, shelves, and tables clean. When boxes are overflowing from shelves and art supplies are jam-packed into drawers, children inevitably will clean up by simply shoving and stuffing materials back into crowded spaces. Also, dust gathers easily in a classroom stuffed with furniture and neglected stacks of files, papers, articles, magazines, and books. This presents a health problem, especially for the growing number of children and adults who have asthma. See the box on the next page for ideas for eliminating clutter in the classroom.

Four Ways to Eliminate Clutter in the Classroom

1. Remove unnecessary furniture and materials using the criteria listed in Chapter Two, "Deciding What's Essential: Criteria for Furniture, Materials, and Storage Space."

2. Use the "Two-Year Rule" and "Two-Inch Rule" to reduce and eliminate paper clutter.

Two-Year Rule: If you haven't used a teaching material, looked at the periodical sitting in the corner, or referenced an article pinned to your bulletin board for two years, then chances are you won't ever.

Two-Inch Rule: No pile should get higher than two inches. If that pile of papers sitting on your desk grows two inches high, it's time for you to sort, file, and throw away.

3. Use a "Clutter Basket" along with a "Do Now Basket" to manage paper clutter in your personal space. As items come in during the week, make quick judgments as to which basket they belong in. Once a week, sort through the two baskets. If the "do now" items haven't been done yet, complete them. Sort items in the "clutter" basket into the "do now" basket, into files for later attention, or into the trash or recycling bin.

4. Collect and keep children's work in labeled containers. This will help keep the work organized and dust free. It also shows that you value the children's work. Consider keeping a "Finished Work Box" where children put any work that is completed during the day and a "Checked Work Box" where children retrieve work that you've reviewed. Also consider having two separate bins for homework papers, one labeled "Homework In" and the other labeled "Homework Out."

Make cleaning up as easy as possible.

As you arrange the classroom, take measures to make cleaning up as easy as possible. Here are some suggestions:

- *Purchase several sets of cleaning tools such as brooms, dustpans, rug or floor sweepers, and damp mops.* Keep them in different locations of the room and near areas where students will most likely use them, to provide easy and quick access.

- *Place receptacles for trash and recycling in many locations of the room.* Practice good recycling habits and teach students to do the same.

- *Keep a supply of newspapers, plastic sheeting, and other materials for protecting furniture.* Put these near the messier art supplies, such as glue, paint, and clay.

- *Keep a supply of empty plastic bins with lids that children can use to store ongoing projects.* This cuts down on clutter and teaches children how to be organized and how to care for work.

Of course, making cleaning tools accessible to children is only half the equation. Children also have to be taught how to clean thoroughly. This means modeling the skills for them and giving them plenty of opportunities to practice, make mistakes, and try again. Expecting children to do a thorough job with cleaning not only keeps the classroom healthy, but teaches children to be responsible and to care for their environment.

Be an Advocate for an Environmentally Healthy School

The final step you can take in creating a healthy school is to continually educate yourself, colleagues, custodians, and students' families about potential environmental health problems and solutions. With wide community awareness and support, you'll have a much better chance of creating a healthy environment for students and yourself. Common school-wide issues that you might want to address include the following:

- Using safe cleaning products in the bathrooms, hallways, and cafeteria.
- Using safe (low or no VOC—volatile organic compounds) paint and floor wax in classrooms and community spaces.

- Removing wall-to-wall carpeting when it shows signs of mold and mildew.

- Maintaining the school-wide heating, cooling, and ventilation systems to eliminate bacteria and mold.

- Using vacuum cleaners with high efficiency particulate air (HEPA) filters to clean the entire school, thus helping to minimize allergens overall.

- Moving idling buses to areas away from the school.

Below are excellent resources for educating yourself about the health and safety hazards in classrooms and schools:

Healthy Schools Network, Inc.
96 South Swan Street, Albany, NY 12210
Phone: 518-462-0632
Fax: 518-462-0433
www.hsnet.org
Email: askhealthyschls@aol.com

A clearinghouse of information for educators and families, this nonprofit organization offers a wealth of practical information for improving indoor air quality and making schools safer and healthier for children and adults. There are many good publications available on their website. Others can be ordered at a minimal cost.

Institute for Children's Environmental Health
P.O. Box 757, Langley, WA 98260
Phone: 360-221-7995
Fax: 360-221-7993
www.iceh.org and www.partnersforchildren.org
Email: emiller@iceh.org

This nonprofit educational organization works to ensure a healthy, just, and sustainable future for children. The primary mission of ICEH is "to foster collaborative initiatives to mitigate environmental exposures that can undermine the health of current and future generations."

Healthy Kids—The Key to Basics
Contact: Ellie Goldberg, MEd., Educational Rights Specialist
79 Elmore Street, Newton, MA 02459-1137
Phone: 617-965-9637
www.breatheamerica.com/common/resourcelist.htm
Email: ERG_HK@JUNO.COM

This information and consulting service promotes health and educational equity for students with asthma, allergies, and other chronic health conditions. Healthy Kids offers a wide range of low-cost information packets and consulting services to individuals, schools, health professionals, and organizations. All of these resources are listed on the organization's website.

Be an Advocate for a Healthy School

The United States Environmental Protection Agency (EPA)

The agency offers many valuable resources for educators, including:

- "Tools for Schools" self-help kit. The EPA created this self-help kit because so many schools have indoor air quality problems that can be resolved easily and at low cost with the assistance of school personnel. National sponsors of the kit include the EPA, American Federation of Teachers, National Education Association, National PTA, American Lung Association, and others. The kit can be ordered from the EPA by calling 202-512-1800 or faxing 202-512-2250.

- "Indoor Air Quality and Student Performance." This flyer gives a good overview of how indoor air quality affects children's ability to learn and cites effects from building-related illnesses. The flyer is available at www.epa.gov/iaq/schools.

In Parting

LESSONS FROM
THE CLUTTER QUEEN

*O*NCE UPON A TIME *there was a teacher who had accumulated so many materials in her classroom that she began to call herself the "Clutter Queen." Teaching materials were stuffed into the closets, stacked on every flat surface, and falling off the shelves. The classroom cried out for rearrangement of work areas, desks, shelves, and closets, and sorely needed a larger meeting area. Worst of all, the teacher didn't know where to begin.*

Finally, she decided to focus on one goal at a time, with a plan to use small steps to reach each goal. The first week she picked one small area of the classroom—a shelf for games—to clear of clutter, discarding some items, putting others in a storage box for later consideration, and reorganizing the remaining ones. After the first week she saw a dramatic effect. As soon as she had cleared and rearranged the shelf, children began to use materials they hadn't touched all year. They also took better care of what was there. Encouraged, she repeated the process in another area the next week.

While this may sound like a fairy tale, it's not. I have met this teacher and have seen her success. Her story has a happy ending. What about yours? Now that you have thought about the impact of the physical arrangement of the classroom, the hard part begins. There you stand, class list in hand, surrounded by furniture and supplies, faced with putting your educational beliefs and goals into the real practice of setting up the classroom. How do you begin to make your vision a reality? In parting, I offer three final thoughts.

Small, Simple Changes Can Have Dramatic Effects

Often when we think about redesigning a classroom, we feel overwhelmed. Our first instinct is to think that we must totally overhaul the room. This happens especially if the problem we are trying to solve feels big. So here is the first most important idea to keep in mind: Small, simple changes can have dramatic effects. What does this mean?

First, as you think about redesigning a classroom, it is often just as effective to take small steps as it is to rearrange the whole classroom at once. While it's important to start with a large-scale plan, this plan can be achieved over the course of a year, or even two! Going slowly at first and taking one small step at a time can provide important results for the children and feel satisfying to you. Rather than trying to tackle everything at once, focus on one area of a classroom and arrange it thoroughly and thoughtfully.

Second, invite colleagues to help you. If the problem seems complicated, there is a tendency to look for a complex solution even though the answer could be quite simple. Often we are too enmeshed in the problem ourselves to see the simple fix or to know the small steps that will help us most. Let a colleague or friend help you analyze the problem and look for solutions. While this can feel uncomfortable at first, this set of outside eyes can be very helpful, both in suggesting design changes and in recognizing organization elements that are working well.

Lessons from the Clutter Queen

Be Flexible

There are many elements to consider in designing a classroom and many ways we can accomplish change. All classrooms have organization problems. I've found that one of the most critical ingredients to solving these problems and creating a vital classroom design is having a positive, flexible attitude. If something doesn't work the first time around, it's important to be able to recognize this, shift gears, and try again. There's no one right way to design a classroom. Each classroom presents many possibilities for design, and with each new possibility there is the chance for success or failure. Staying flexible and open-minded and being able to view failure as a chance for more creative thinking is essential.

Share Ownership with Students

The final element that I believe affects the success of any classroom design is how we view the ownership of the room. When we truly believe that the classroom belongs to both the teacher and the students, then, and only then, will the design ultimately be successful. The room and the teacher's language must reflect this shared ownership. Even a classroom that has many obstacles can become an effective environment when the teacher considers the needs of the students and invites their input into decisions about how to arrange furniture, organize materials, display work, and use and care for the room. The classroom is the working and living environment for both teachers and children. Its design and organization will be most effective when the teacher's attitude, beliefs, and actions honor that collaboration.

So, start small, but start with a plan. Be prepared to change your plan. And involve students in helping you create the best arrangement possible. Good luck and have fun!

In Parting

Appendix A

Suggested Materials List for Grades K-6

The following list provides an overview of recommended learning materials for kindergarten through sixth grade classrooms. It is a general list, not intended to be exhaustive.

Each area of learning includes two categories:

1. Equipment: purchased items that remain in the class over a long period of time

2. Supplies: purchased or found items that are used and replaced

Reading and Language Arts

Equipment:

- rich variety of books for a class library including fiction, nonfiction, poetry, magazines, and comic books
- dictionary, thesaurus, encyclopedia, almanac, etc.
- teacher read-aloud books
- children's individual published books, class-made experience books, and if possible, a machine to make spiral-bound books
- multiple copies of trade books
- broad collection of fiction and non-fiction in big book form for K–2 classrooms
- quality tape recorder with 2–4 sets of earphones and a collection of music tapes, book/tape sets, and blank tapes for children's recording
- language arts games providing practice in reading, phonics, sight words, spelling, vocabulary, and grammar specific to grade and ability level
- large and small chalkboards or dry-erase boards
- flannel board, flannel letters and story props, and magnetic boards and letters for K–3 classrooms
- letter stamps and stencils
- overhead projector
- 2–4 computer stations based on grade level

Supplies:

- materials for children to make their own games (old game boards, cardboard, dice and spinners, index cards, buttons, small polished stones, and old game markers)
- paper in a variety of sizes, colors, and types (construction, lined, story, cards, art, etc.)
- variety of drawing and writing tools including both fat and thin widths in K–2 classrooms
- pencil grips and lots of good erasers in K–2
- materials to make and fasten books
- interactive and creative computer software

Suggested Materials List for Grades K–6

Drama

Equipment:

- props, dress-ups, and furniture for dramatizations of stories and social studies and history themes. Examples of topics at different grade levels include:

  K–2: house and home life, school life, community services like the post office, grocery store, hospital, etc.

  Grades 3–6: Native American life, immigration, life in other countries, a time in history, etc.

- puppets, puppetry props, and puppet-show curtain

Supplies:

- paper and cardboard
- non-hardening modeling clay
- crayons, pencils, markers, and chalk
- chalkboard and dry-erase board
- materials to make puppets (paper bags, craft sticks, old socks, oaktag, etc.)

Art

Equipment:

- large rectangular table for big projects and oilcloth cover for protection

- painting easel and smocks (K–3)
- paint cups and a wide variety of brushes
- pegboard, rack, or line for drying
- shelves for drying, storage, and display
- stamps and stencils
- rulers and hole punches
- variety of quality scissors, including decorative edgers
- brayers and printing plates

Supplies:

- drawing tools in a variety of styles and colors, including markers, crayons (wax, Cray-pas and Payons), pastels, and charcoal
- variety of paints, watercolors, and colored ink pads
- variety of lead and colored pencils
- non-hardening and hardening modeling clay
- variety of tapes, glue, and other fasteners
- collage and project materials including string, fabric, buttons, pipe cleaners, yarn, wood pieces, cotton and cotton swabs, craft sticks, toothpicks, straws, candle wax, and sponges
- "found" materials from nature and industry (boxes, newspaper, cardboard, styrofoam)

Appendix A

Art Supplies Specific to Grades 4–6

- sewing, knitting, crocheting, and other handcraft materials
- Plaster of Paris
- calligraphy and ink pens
- wood cutting materials

Construction (K–3)

Equipment:

- hardwood unit blocks in many sizes and shapes, and if possible, a large or jumbo set so many children can be building at the same time and constructions can remain intact over several days

- accessories for unit block work (proportionally-sized) including:
  - doll-house furniture, small tabletop blocks, and an assortment of small wooden pieces from a furniture woodshop
  - bendable multicultural dolls including families and community workers
  - farm and zoo animals
  - cars, trucks, and other vehicles
  - Lego blocks and other materials for building and model-making such as Kapla blocks
  - pulleys, "S" hooks, and clamps

Supplies:

- non-hardening modeling clay in wide variety of colors
- wire, string, pipe cleaners, straws
- masking tape to adhere things to the unit blocks
- "found" materials like shells, buttons, scraps of material, cardboard tubes, sticks, etc.
- paper, oaktag, and drawing and writing tools

Suggested Materials List for Grades K–6

Geography (Grades 3–6)

Equipment:

- globes
- variety of maps, including topography maps
- stream table
- atlas
- water pump
- compasses
- a variety of rulers

Supplies:

- supplies for making maps such as poster board, Plaster of Paris, and wire
- plastic tubing and connectors
- clean sand
- clear plastic sheeting

Math and Science

Equipment:

- sturdy sand/water table with wheels on two legs, good quality liner, and a drain
- a variety of equipment for sand/water table including the following: different sizes and shapes of spoons, cups, dishes, bottles, cans, and pans; sponges; buckets; plastic tubing and connectors; funnels; and pumps
- one (minimum) rectangular table for on-going science exhibits and discovery work
- variety of equipment for science table including:
  - aquariums and other containers to hold living (plants and animals) and nonliving things
  - microscope, magnifying glasses, and hand lens
  - mirrors
  - measuring devices
  - magnets and metal materials (both magnetic and non-magnetic)
  - balances, weights, and pulleys
  - tweezers, eye droppers, and probes
- games and manipulatives appropriate to age and ability level. Examples include attribute and pattern blocks, checkers, chess, playing cards, cribbage, marbles and marble game mat, pick-up sticks, geoblocks and cards, tangrams, geoboards, fraction squares, Cuisenaire rods, Unifix Cubes, Mancala, Connect Four, and Uno
- child-made math and science games
- non-fiction math and science books
- 2–4 computer stations based on grade level

Appendix A

Supplies

- variety of supplies for sand/water table including:
  - clean, fine, nontoxic sand, dried beans, and peas
  - fresh, clean water (changed daily)
  - food coloring and cornstarch for use with water

- non-hardening modeling clay and weights

- "found" materials that float or sink

■ variety of items for math and science study including rocks, shells, plants and seeds, batteries and bulbs, insects, small reptiles and amphibians, fish, birds, small mammals, science and math kits obtained from science museums, etc.

■ materials for children to make their own games (old game boards, cardboard, dice and spinners, index cards, buttons, small polished stones, and old game markers)

■ creative and interactive computer software

Indoor Movement and Music

Suggested
Materials List
for Grades
K–6

Equipment:

- hoops and cones

- scarves and ribbons

- bean bags and various bean bag targets

- soft velcro darts and target

- variety of soft balls

- mats for floor activities and games

- various timers

- chalkboard and dry-erase board

- CD player and variety of music for listening and movement/dance

- rhythm and music instruments

Appendix B

Materials for the Whole-Group Meeting Area

Blackboard or Dry-Erase Board

Teachers use blackboards and dry-erase boards in the meeting area for writing, drawing, and recording anything that doesn't have to be saved for a long time. Some teachers use them to list the daily schedule and some use them for various sign-ups such as attendance, lunch choice, academic work choice, or sharing in Morning Meeting. Parts of the blackboard can be used for display as well.

Choosing boards:

- Many classrooms now are equipped with permanent dry-erase boards instead of blackboards. While dry-erase boards are easy to clean, many of the dry-erase markers contain solvents that are harmful to breathe. If you're going to use a dry-erase board, be sure to use the nontoxic, odor free, dry-erase markers that have recently come on the market.

- If there are no permanent blackboards or dry-erase boards in the meeting area, use smaller portable ones. Portable boards come in various sizes. Pick one that can sit well on the chart stand lip or against the front of the chart stand. Be sure it can be stored in the meeting area so it is always there when needed. You can also make your own dry-erase board by purchasing melamine-coated Masonite, available at any lumberyard, and cutting it to the size you want.

Box Benches

A box bench is a moveable rectangular box that up to four children can sit on. Children can also lean against the bench for back support when sitting on the floor. The bench is light enough for one or two children to move, making it useful in creating a small group setting.

Making box benches:

- These boxes are relatively easy and inexpensive for someone with basic carpentry skills to build. The bench is usually 14" wide, 10" high and up to 4' long. The boxes have open bottoms. The four sides are cut from 1" x 10" pine; the top is made from 5/8" plywood. The entire structure is fastened together with sheetrock screws with their heads countersunk. The top of the box is then covered with a piece of rug, which overlaps the front and the back sides (but not the ends) by about four inches. The rug may be stapled or tacked to the sides.

Bulletin Board

Permanent bulletin boards are often used for displays in the meeting area. Smaller portable bulletin boards, which children can carry, can also work quite well. These can either be purchased or handmade.

Making a bulletin board:

- If you are making a bulletin board, use particleboard covered with flame-retardant material or a piece of Masonite, which tends to be thinner, less bulky and usually lighter than particleboard. However, Masonite cannot be used with pushpins. Either material can be purchased at most lumberyards.

- You can lean a portable bulletin board against a wall in the meeting area or attach it to the wall or the chart stand with Velcro. After the meeting, you can display it in another part of the classroom where it could serve as a reference.

Chime or Bell to Signal for Quiet

Many teachers use a chime, bell, or other instrument to signal children to "stop, look, and listen." When the teacher rings the chime or bell, all children stop what they're doing and give their attention to the teacher.

Choosing and storing chimes or bells:

- Have more than one chime or bell so you can get to one quickly and easily no matter where you are in the room. Many teachers always keep one chime or bell in the meeting area.

- Make sure that the sound is clear and loud enough for children to hear without being too loud and piercing for sensitive ears. See Appendix D for a source of quality chimes and bells.

CD/Tape Player

A tape or a CD player can be a very useful teaching tool. Many teachers use them most frequently in the meeting area.

**Materials
for the
Whole-Group
Meeting Area**

Choosing and storing a CD/tape player:

- Invest in a good tape or CD player. The quality of the sound is important to using this tool effectively.

- Store a CD or tape player where it is protected from accidental bumping and jostling, yet allows for easy access during meetings and lessons. A shelf or windowsill near the chart stand or a shelf tucked behind the chart stand is ideal, provided these locations are close to electrical outlets.

Clipboards

These are essential to the success of many lessons in the meeting area. They provide a hard surface for children to write on and can also define individual working spaces when children are using materials such as math manipulatives. Every child should have a clipboard.

Appendix B

Making and storing clipboards:

- If clipboards are too expensive to purchase, try using very heavy cardboard or Masonite with a clothespin or binder clip.

- Some teachers also make "workboards" out of Masonite. Workboards are a larger version of a clipboard (generally between 12"x 18" and 24"x 24") but without the clip. They provide a good surface for working with math manipulatives and big art or writing projects.

- Many teachers store clipboards and workboards in milk crates placed on the floor in the meeting area or on a shelf nearby.

Easel Chart Stand

An essential tool for teaching in the meeting area, chart stands can be purchased through most school supply catalogues. See Appendix D for recommendations.

Choosing and storing chart stands:

When purchasing a chart stand, consider:
- *The height of the easel:* Children must be able to write comfortably on the chart while standing.

- *The sturdiness:* Since the chart stand takes a prominent place in the meeting area and is used frequently, it should stand sturdily and provide a very firm surface for writing.

- *The design of the lip:* The lip should be wide enough and flat enough to hold various writing tools and additional charts and writing boards.

- *The storage potential:* In most classrooms, the chart stand is kept in the meeting area to define the gathering spot. However, if you need a large unobstructed space in the meeting area, make sure the chart stand can be folded flat and set safely against a wall.

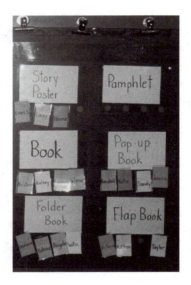

Permanent Planning Board

Many teachers keep a permanent planning board in the meeting area which children use to make choices during the day. For example, the planning board might list the various choices available during a "Reading/Writing Workshop" or an "Academic Choice" time. Students indicate their choice by attaching a nametag to one of the items (see photographs).

There are many ways to make a planning board depending on how you will use it in the classroom. Some list activities or materials available during a particular time of the day, some list choices within a content area, and some list several periods of the day that children plan for. Most important is that the labels on the board can be easily changed so that it can be used in a variety of ways.

Making and storing a permanent planning board:

Essentially you want to create a grid listing the choices available and a set of name cards for children to attach to the grid. There are many materials that can be used to create a planning board. To make the board itself, you can use painted plywood, fabric-covered Homasote, heavy cardboard, or laminated poster board. A permanent marker can be used to make the grid. To create simple name cards, print

each child's name on a clothespin, tongue depressor, round piece of oaktag, or square veneer sample with a hole. Pushpins, hooks, and various kinds of clips work well to attach the nametags to the board.

Here are four specific options for creating a permanent planning board:

- Use a piece of white, melamine-coated Masonite for the board and create the grid with bookbinding tape, allowing you to easily remove strips and re-create new grid areas. Place at least two adhesive strips of "loop" Velcro in each grid opening (again, they can be easily removed). One is for the label naming the choice and the other is to hold the children's names. Make labels and several name cards for each child with "hook" Velcro attached to the back. Store name cards in a box large enough for children to easily find their names, or hang the name cards in alphabetical order on Velcro strips attached to a smaller "Name Card Board." This type of planning board can be attached to a wall or bookcase or leaned against the lip of a blackboard or chart stand.

- Use a piece of sheet metal—taping the edges for safety—or a factory-made magnetic board for the planning board. As in the previous example, create a grid using bookbinding tape or strips of magnetic tape. Create labels and name cards with magnetic tape or magnetic clips for attaching to the board. Store name cards as in the example above.

- Hang a "sentence strip chart" on a wall, bulletin board, or bookcase. Children place their names in one of the strips to make a choice. Use colored oaktag to make the labels and name cards. Another option for name cards is to use photographs of the children.

- Laminate a heavy piece of poster board and attach "library book pockets" to create the grid of options. Use mounting putty to attach the pockets and the labels so they can be removed and changed easily. Another possibility is to simply write the choice directly on the pockets since they are inexpensive and can be ordered in large quantities. Create a set of name sticks for each child using tongue depressors that can be slipped into the pockets.

Rugs

A rug in the meeting area can help define the space, make the area feel warm and inviting, and enable children to sit comfortably on the floor. There are several important considerations when deciding what kind and size of rug to get.

Choosing a rug:

- Most classes will need a rug larger than the standard 8'x10' or 9'x12' rug, to provide enough room for children to sit comfortably, legs crossed or in chairs, in a true circle. I recommend about 2' of space per average-sized eight- to ten-year-old, so a 12'x12' rug would be suitable for twenty children this age.

- The rug should have bound edges to keep it from fraying. A rug with a dense, low pile is easier for students to work on. If you're putting the rug on bare floor, get a non-skid mat to go underneath so the rug doesn't slide. The mat also adds a little padding for warmth and comfort.

- Choose a plain, bright, solid color for the meeting area rug. While school catalogues often carry rugs with very colorful alphabet, number, and game board patterns, most of these rugs are too visually busy for the purposes of a meeting space.

- Choose a rug that's easy to clean. As discussed in Chapter Seven, it's essential to keep rugs in the classroom clean.

Materials for the Whole-Group Meeting Area

Appendix C

Art Materials and Projects Suitable for Children
and Other High Risk Individuals

This table appeared in the chapter on classroom safety in *The Artist's Complete Health and Safety Guide* (Allworth Press, 1994). It is reprinted here with permission from the publisher and the author, Monona Rossol. For more information or to order this book, contact:

Allworth Press
10 East 23rd Street, Suite 510
New York, New York 10010
Phone: 212-777-8395
www.allworth.com

Appendix C

Art Materials and Projects Suitable for Children

TABLE 29	Art Materials and Projects Suitable for Children and Other High Risk Individuals
DO NOT USE	SUBSTITUTES
SOLVENTS & SOLVENT-CONTAINING PRODUCTS	WATER-BASED & SOLVENT-FREE PRODUCTS
Alkyd, oil enamels, or other solvent-containing paints	Use acrylics, oil sticks, colors, water containing paints, or other water-based paints containing safe pigments.
Turpentine, paint thinners, citrus turps, or other solvents for cleaning up or thinning artist's oil paints.	Mix oil-based, solvent-free paints with linseed oil only. Clean with baby oil followed by soap and water. Choose paints containing safe pigments.
Solvent-based silk screen inks and other printing inks containing solvents or requiring solvents for clean up.	Use water-based silk screen inks, block printing, or stencil inks with safe pigments.
Solvent-containing varnishes, mediums, and alcohol-containing shellacs.	Use acrylic emulsion coatings, or the teacher can apply it for students under proper conditions.
Rubber cement and thinners for paste up and mechanicals.	Use low temperature wax methods, double sided tape, glue sticks, or other solvent-free materials.
Airplane glue and other solvent-containing glues	Use white glue, school paste, glue sticks, preservative-free wheat paste, or other solvent-free glues.
Permanent felt-tip markers, white board markers and other solvent-containing markers.	Use water-based markers.

DO NOT USE	SUBSTITUTES
POWDERED OR DUSTY MATERIALS	DUSTLESS PRODUCTS/PROCESSES
Clay dust from mixing dry clay, sanding greenware, and other dusty processes.	Purchase talc-free, low silica, pre-mixed clay. Trim clay when leather hard, clean up often during work, and practice good hygiene and dust control.
Ceramic glaze dust from mixing ingredients, glazing, and other processes.	Substitute with paints or buy glazes free of lead and other toxic metals which are premixed, or mix in local exhaust ventilation system. Control dust carefully.
Metal enamel dust.	Substitute with paints. Even lead-free enamels may contain other very toxic metals. Avoid enamels also because heat and acids are used.
Powdered tempera and other powdered paints.	Purchase premixed paints or have the teacher mix them. Use paints with safe ingredients.
Powdered dyes for batik, tie dyeing, and other processes.	Use vegetable and plant materials (e.g. onion skins, tea, etc.) and approved food dyes (e.g. unsweetened Kool-Aid).
Plaster dust.	Have the teacher premix the plaster outdoors or in local exhaust ventilation. Do not sand plaster or do other dusty work. Do not cast hands or other body parts to avoid burns. Cut rather than tear plaster impregnated casting cloth.
Instant papier mache dust from finely ground magazines, newspapers, etc.	Use pieces of plain paper or black and white newspaper with white glue paste, or other safe glues.

Appendix C

Art Materials and Projects Suitable for Children

DO NOT USE	SUBSTITUTES
Pastels, chalks or dry markers which create dust.	Use oil pastels or sticks, crayons, and dustless chalks.
AEROSOLS AND SPRAY PRODUCTS	**LIQUID MATERIALS**
Spray paints, fixatives, etc.	Use water-based liquids which are brushed, dripped, or splattered on or have the teacher use sprays in local exhaust ventilation or out doors.
Air brushes.	Replace with other paint methods. Mist should not be inhaled and air brushes can be misused.
MISCELLANEOUS PRODUCTS	SUBSTITUTES
All types of professional artist's materials.	Use only products approved and recommended for children when teaching either children or adults who require very special protection.
Toxic metals such as arsenic, lead, cadmium, lithium, barium, chrome, nickel, vanadium, manganese, antimony, and more.	These are common ingredients in ceramic glazes, enamels, paints, and many art materials. Use only materials found free of highly toxic substances.
Epoxy resins, instant glues, and other plastic resin adhesives.	Use white glue, library paste, glue sticks or other safe adhesives.
Plastic resin casting systems or preformed plastic materials.	Do not do plastic resin casting or use any plastic material in ways that release vapors, gases, or odors.
Acid etches and pickling baths.	Do no do projects that use these.
Bleach for reverse dying of fabric or colored paper.	Do no do projects using bleach. Thinned white paint can be used to simulate bleach on colored paper.

DO NOT USE	SUBSTITUTES
Photographic chemicals.	Use blueprint paper to make sun grams or use Polaroid cameras. Be sure students do not abuse Polaroid film or pictures which contain toxic chemicals.

MISCELLANEOUS PRODUCTS	SUBSTITUTES
Stained glass projects.	Do not do projects using lead, solder or glass cutting. Use colored cellophane and black paper or tape to simulate stained glass.
Industrial talcs contaminated with asbestos or nonfibrous asbestos minerals used in many white clays, slip casting clays, glazes, French chalk, and parting powders.	Always order talc-free products.
Sculpture stones contaminated with asbestos such as some soapstones, steatites, serpentines, etc.	Always use stones found free of asbestos on analysis.
Art paints and markers used to decorate the skin (e.g., clown faces).	Always use products approved for use on the skin (e.g., cosmetics or colored zinc sun-screen creams).
Scented markers.	Do not use with children. It encourages them to sniff and taste art materials. They are acceptable for older visually impaired students for distinguishing colors.
Plants and seeds.	Check identity of all plants to be sure no toxic or sensitizing plants are used (e.g., poison oak, castor beans).

Appendix C

DO NOT USE	SUBSTITUTES
Donated, found, or old materials whose ingredients are unknown.	Do not use these materials unless investigation identifies the ingredients and they are found safe.
Products with possible biological hazards.	Use clean, unused materials. Products used with food or other animal or organic materials may harbor bacteria or other hazardous microbes (e.g., washed plastic meat trays may harbor salmonella).

Art Materials and Projects Suitable for Children

Appendix D

Recommended Sources for Classroom Furniture and Supplies

Animal Town

PO Box 757, Greenland, NH 03840

800-445-8642 animaltown.com

- *Cooperative board games*
- *Toys, books, and crafts*

Bender-Burkot

PO Box 147, Pollocksville, NC 28573

800-682-2638 bender-burkot.com

- *Great prices on chart paper*

Childcraft Education Corp.

PO Box 3239, Lancaster, PA 17604

800-631-5652 childcraft.com

- *High-quality unit block sets*
- *Sturdy sand and water tables*
- *Tables and chairs*

Community Playthings

PO Box 901, Route 213, Rifton, NY 12471

800-777-4244 communityplaythings.com

- *High-quality hardwood furniture*
- *Modular lofts requiring no construction*
- *The best in hardwood unit building blocks and accessories*
- *Versatile furniture for dramatization*
- *Great cubbies which they call "Tote Boxes"*

Crazy Creek Products

PO Box 1050, Red Lodge, MT 59068

800-331-0304 crazycreek.com

- *Durable floor chairs and cushions*

Creative Publications

5040 West 111th Street, Oak Lawn, IL 60453

800-624-0822 creativepublications.com

- *Great math manipulatives and games*

Cuisenaire

PO Box 5040, White Plains, NY 10602-5040

877-411-2761 cuisenaire.com

- *Wonderful variety of versatile math and science materials*

Delta Education

PO Box 3000, Nashua, NH 03061-3000

800-442-5444 delta-education.com

- *Wide variety of science and math materials*

Recommended Sources for Classroom Furniture and Supplies

Developmental Studies Center

2000 Embarcadero, Suite 305, Oakland, CA 94606-5300

800-666-7270 devstu.org

- *Excellent grade-level (K–8) books— including a wide variety of literature— that address ethical and social issues*

Dick Blick Co.

PO Box 1267, Galesburg, IL 61402-1267

800-447-8192 dickblick.com

- *Good art materials, reasonably priced*
- *Decorative scissors for primary grade children's displays*

ETA

500 Greenview Court, Vernon Hills, IL 60061-1862

800-445-5985 etauniverse.com

- *Several catalogues available, including ones for math and science materials*
- *Math catalogue offers a large assortment of manipulatives*

Frey Scientific

PO Box 8105, 100 Paragon Parkway, Mansfield, OH 44903

800-225-3739 freyscientific.com

- *Huge selection of science materials*

Gopher Sport

PO Box 998, Owatanna, MN 55060

800-533-0446 gophersport.com

- *Wide variety of indoor and outdoor movement, fitness, and games equipment*

J. L. Hammett Co.

One Paliotti Parkway, Lyons, NY 14489

800-333-4600 hammett.com

- *Sturdy, wooden chart stands*
- *Sturdy, metal chart stands that are adjustable and include storage bins*
- *Wide variety of art supplies, including nontoxic rubber cement, mounting putty, and multicultural modeling clay*
- *Wide variety of classroom materials, including multicultural dolls and puppets*
- *Storage "milk crates" and storage units on wheels*

Kaplan Companies

PO Box 609, Lewisville, NC 27023-0609

800-334-2014 kaplanco.com

- *Excellent variety of classroom materials and supplies*
- *Multicultural crayons and paints*

Lakeshore Learning Materials

2695 E. Dominguez Street, Carson, CA 90749

800-421-5354 lakeshorelearning.com

- *People Colors markers, crayons, and paints*
- *Multicultural puppet families and dolls*
- *Career puppets*
- *Accessories for unit building blocks*

McGraw-Hill Children's Publishing

3195 Wilson Drive NW, Grand Rapids, MI 49544

800-845-8149 instructionalfair.com

- *Math manipulatives*
- *General classroom supplies*

NASCO

PO Box 901, Fort Atkinson, WI 53538-0901

800-558-9595 nascofa.com

- *Good variety of reasonably-priced classroom supplies,
  especially construction materials and large motor indoor materials*
- *Sturdy, metal chart stands that are adjustable and include storage bins*
- *Decorative scissors, singles and in sets—excellent for making displays*

Recommended Sources for Classroom Furniture and Supplies

Quill

100 Schelter Road, Lincolnshire, IL 60069-3621

800-789-7020 quill.com

- *Office supply mega-store with great pricing*

The Rainbow Collection

PO Box 754, Milldale, CT 06467

888-371-3137

- *Rubber stamp sets, board games, puppets, etc.*

Sax Arts & Crafts

2405 S. Calhoun Road, New Berlin, WI 53151

800-558-6696 saxarts.com

- *Wonderful variety of art supplies (discounts on bulk buying),
  including wide array of multicultural materials*

School Specialty, Inc.

PO Box 1579, Appleton, WI 54913-1579

888-388-3224 schoolspecialty.com

- *Tables and chairs*
- *Wide variety of supplies at reasonable prices*

Solutions

PO Box 6878, Portland, OR 97228-6878

800-342-9988 solutionscatalog.com
- *Variety of cushioned floor seats*
- *Large floor pillows*
- *Storage pockets for doors*

Sportime Elementary

One Sportime Way, Atlanta, GA 30340

800-283-5700 sportime.com
- *Wide variety of indoor and outdoor movement, fitness, and games equipment*
- *Adapted physical education equipment, innovative movement and game materials for children with disabilities*

Steps to Literacy

PO Box 6263, Bridgewater, NJ 08807

800-895-2804 stepstoliteracy.com
- *Materials for setting up a reading area*

Teaching Resource Center

730 Design Court, Suite 405, Thula Vista, CA 91911

800-833-3389 trcabc.com
- *Classroom furniture*
- *Dry-erase boards*

U.S. Games

Three locations: Central (address given below), Northeast, and West

P.O. Box 117028, Carrollton, TX 75011-7028

800-327-0484 us-games.com
- *Wide variety of indoor and outdoor movement, fitness, and games equipment*
- *Sole provider of Huffy equipment*

West Music

PO Box 5521, Coralville, IA 52241

800-397-9378   westmusic.com

- *Chimes and bells with excellent tones, including the highly recommended Earth Bell— Order #BEWB174*

Recommended Sources for Classroom Furniture and Supplies

Appendix E

Child Development:

A Selected Bibliography

A to Z Guide to Your Child's Behavior: A Parent's Easy and Authoritative Reference to Hundreds of Everyday Problems and Concerns from Birth to 12 Years. Compiled by the faculty of the Children's National Medical Center, under the direction of David Mrazek, M.D., and William Garrison, Ph.D., with Laura Elliott. New York: Pedigree Books, 1993.

Ages and Stages: Developmental Descriptions & Activities, Birth Through Eight Years. Karen Miller. Chelsea, MA: Teleshare Publishing Company, 1985.

Black Children: Their Roots, Culture, and Learning Styles. Janice E. Hale-Benson. Baltimore, MD: The Johns Hopkins University Press, 1982.

Child Behavior: The Classic Childcare Manual from the Gesell Institute of Human Development. Francis L. Ilg, M.D., Louise Bates Ames, Ph.D., and Sidney M. Baker, M.D. New York: Harperperennial Library, 1992.

Childhood: A Multicultural View. Melvin Konner. Boston, MA: Little, Brown & Co., 1991.

Contexts for Learning: Sociocultural Dynamics in Children's Development. Edited by Ellice A. Forman, Norris Minick, and C. Addison Stone. New York: Oxford University Press, 1993.

How Is My First Grader Doing In School? Jennifer Richard Jacobson. New York: Simon & Schuster, 1998. First in a series of six books. Entire series (grades 1–6) is in print.

Teaching Ten to Fourteen Year Olds. Chris Stevenson. White Plains, NY: Longman Publishing Group, 1992.

Theories of Development: Concepts and Applications. William C. Crain. Englewood Cliffs, NJ: Prentice-Hall Inc., 1980.

Touchpoints: Your Child's Emotional and Behavioral Development. T. Berry Brazelton. Reading, MA: Addison Wesley Publishing Co., 1992.

Yardsticks: Children in the Classroom Ages 4–14. Chip Wood. Greenfield, MA: Northeast Foundation for Children, 1997.

Your Ten to Fourteen Year Old. Louise Bates Ames, Ph.D., Frances L. Ilg, M.D., and Sidney Baker, M.D. New York: Delacorte Press, 1988.

**Child
Development:
A Selected
Bibliography**

REFERENCES

Charney, Ruth S. *Teaching Children to Care: Management in the Responsive Classroom.* Greenfield, MA: Northeast Foundation for Children, 1991.

Gesell, Dr. Arnold, Dr. Frances L. Ilg and Glenna E. Bullis. *Vision: Its Development in Infant & Child.* Santa Ana, CA: Optometric Extension Program Foundation, 1998.

Healthy Schools Network. "Healthier Cleaning and Maintenance: Practices and Products for Schools." Albany, NY: Healthy Schools Network, Inc., 1999.

Jensen, Eric. "How Julie's Brain Learns." *Educational Leadership,* Vol. 56 No. 3 (November 1998): 41–46.

Kriete, Roxann. *The Morning Meeting Book.* Greenfield, MA: Northeast Foundation for Children, 1998.

Massachusetts Coalition for Occupational Safety and Health (MassCOSH). "Carpeting: Is it a Healthy Choice for Schools?" Jamaica Plain, MA: MassCOSH, 1996.

Rossol, Monona. *The Artist's Complete Health and Safety Guide.* Second Edition. New York: Allworth Press, 1994.

Service Employees International Union, AFL-CIO, CLC. "VDT Health and Safety Fact Sheet." Washington, DC: Service Employees International Union, 1993.

U.S. Department of Labor, Program Highlights. "Safety with Video Display Terminals, Fact Sheet No. 92–94." OSHA Administrative Document, February 17, 1993.

Weinberger, Norman M. "The Music in Our Minds." *Educational Leadership,* Vol. 56, No.3 (November 1998): 36–40.

Wood, Chip. *Yardsticks: Children in the Classroom Ages 4–14.* Greenfield, MA: Northeast Foundation for Children, 1997.

Wood, Chip. *Time to Teach, Time to Learn: Changing the Pace of School.* Greenfield, MA: Northeast Foundation for Children, 1999.

Marlynn K. Clayton has twenty years of experience as a classroom teacher in the primary grades. A co-founder of Northeast Foundation for Children, she has worked for the past eleven years as director of professional development in the consulting teachers branch of the organization. She assists teachers nationwide implementing *The Responsive Classroom®* approach and directs the certification process for educators becoming trainers in *The Responsive Classroom* approach. Marlynn is the author of the video, *Places To Start,* and a co-author of *A Notebook for Teachers.* She has a BA from Smith College and an MEd from the University of Massachusetts.

Mary Beth Forton has been involved in education for eighteen years. She has taught language arts in elementary and middle schools and has worked with students with special needs, grades K–12. She is currently an editor/writer for Northeast Foundation for Children, where she has worked since 1989, and serves as editor of the quarterly publication, *Responsive Classroom: A Newsletter for Teachers.* She has a BA from St. Lawrence University and a Master of Arts in Teaching degree from Brown University.

Jay Lord, a co-founder of Northeast Foundation for Children, currently works in the publishing branch of the organization. He has worked at the foundation for over twenty years as a middle school teacher, workshop presenter, and executive director. Before this, Jay taught and coached sports at the high school and college levels. He has a BA from Amherst College and an MEd from Harvard University and is a co-author of *A Notebook for Teachers.*

ABOUT THE
RESPONSIVE CLASSROOM® APPROACH

This book grew out of the work of Northeast Foundation for Children, Inc. (NEFC) and an approach to teaching known as the *Responsive Classroom* approach. Developed by classroom teachers, this approach consists of highly practical strategies for integrating social and academic learning throughout the school day.

Seven beliefs underlie this approach:

1. The social curriculum is as important as the academic curriculum.

2. How children learn is as important as what they learn: Process and content go hand in hand.

3. The greatest cognitive growth occurs through social interaction.

4. There is a specific set of social skills that children need to learn and practice in order to be successful academically and socially: cooperation, assertion, responsibility, empathy, and self-control.

5. Knowing the children we teach—individually, culturally, and developmentally—is as important as knowing the content we teach.

6. Knowing the families of the children we teach and encouraging their participation is as important as knowing the children we teach.

7. How we, the adults at school, work together to accomplish our shared mission is as important as our individual competence: Lasting change begins with the adult community.

More information and guidance on the *Responsive Classroom* approach are available through:

Publications and Resources

- Books, videos, and audios for K–8 educators
- Website with articles and other information:
  www.responsiveclassroom.org
- Free quarterly newsletter for educators

Professional Development Opportunities

- One-day and week-long workshops for teachers
- Classroom consultations and other services at individual schools and school districts
- Multi-faceted professional development for administrators and all staff at schools wishing to implement the *Responsive Classroom* approach school-wide

For details, contact:

RESPONSIVE CLASSROOM
NORTHEAST FOUNDATION FOR CHILDREN, INC.
85 Avenue A, Suite 204   P.O. Box 718
Turners Falls, MA 01376-0718
Phone 800-360-6332 or 413-863-8288
Fax 877-206-3952
www.responsiveclassroom.org

The Morning Meeting Book

By Roxann Kriete

with contributions by Lynn Bechtel

For K–8 teachers (2002) 228 pages ISBN 978-1-892989-09-3

Use Morning Meeting in your classroom to build community, increase students' investment in learning, and improve academic and social skills. This book features:

■ *Step-by-step guidelines for holding Morning Meeting* ■ *A chapter on Morning Meeting in middle schools* ■ *45 greetings and 66 group activities* ■ *Frequently asked questions and answers*

The First Six Weeks of School

By Paula Denton and Roxann Kriete

For K–6 teachers (2000) 232 pages ISBN 978-1-892989-04-8

Structure the first weeks of school to lay the groundwork for a productive year of learning.

■ *Guidelines for the first six weeks, including daily plans for the first three weeks for grades K–2, grades 3–4, and grades 5–6* ■ *Ideas for building community, teaching routines, introducing engaging curriculum, fostering autonomy* ■ *Games, activities, greetings, songs, read-alouds, and resources especially useful during the early weeks of school*

Classroom Spaces That Work

By Marlynn K. Clayton with Mary Beth Forton

For K–6 teachers (2001) 192 pages ISBN 978-1-892989-05-5

Create a physical environment that is welcoming, well suited to the needs of students and teachers, and conducive to social and academic excellence.

■ *Practical ideas for arranging furniture* ■ *Suggestions for selecting and organizing materials* ■ *Ideas for creating displays* ■ *Guidelines for setting up a meeting area* ■ *Tips for making the space healthy*

Rules in School

By Kathryn Brady, Mary Beth Forton,
Deborah Porter, and Chip Wood

For K–8 teachers (2003) 272 pages ISBN 978-1-892989-10-9

Establish a calm, safe learning environment and teach children self-discipline with this approach to classroom rules.

- *Guidelines for creating rules with students based on their hopes and dreams for school*
- *Steps in modeling and role playing the rules* ■ *How to reinforce the rules through language*
- *Using logical consequences when rules are broken* ■ *Suggestions for teaching children to live by the rules outside the classroom*

Learning Through Academic Choice

By Paula Denton, EdD

For K–6 teachers (2005) 224 pages ISBN 978-1-892989-14-7

Enhance students' learning with this powerful tool for structuring lessons and activities.

- *Information on building a strong foundation for Academic Choice* ■ *Step-by-step look at Academic Choice in action* ■ *Practical advice for creating an Academic Choice lesson plan*
- *Many ideas for Academic Choice activities*

Parents and Teachers Working Together

By Carol Davis and Alice Yang

For K–6 teachers (2005) 232 pages ISBN 978-1-892989-15-4

Build school-home cooperation and involve parents in ways that support their children's learning.

- *Working with diverse family cultures* ■ *Building positive relationships in the early weeks of school* ■ *Keeping in touch all year long* ■ *Involving parents in classroom life, including parents who can't physically come to school* ■ *Problem-solving with parents*